Childhood Autism Spectrum Disorder

Childhood Autism Spectrum Disorder

Evidence-Based Assessment and Intervention

Jessica Glass Kendorski and
Amanda Guld Fisher

MP **MOMENTUM** PRESS
HEALTH

MOMENTUM PRESS, LLC, NEW YORK

Childhood Autism Spectrum Disorder: Evidence-Based Assessment and Intervention

First published in 2018 by
Momentum Press, LLC
222 East 46th Street, New York, NY 10017
www.momentumpress.net

ISBN-13: 978-1-94474-919-4 (paperback)
ISBN-13: 978-1-94474-920-0 (e-book)

Momentum Press Child Clinical Psychology "Nuts and Bolts" Collection

Cover and interior design by Exeter Premedia Services Private Ltd., Chennai, India

First edition: 2018

10 9 8 7 6 5 4 3 2 1

Printed in the United States of America.

Abstract

The evidence-based literature on intervention strategies for students with autism spectrum disorder has mushroomed in the past couple of decades. As the cohort of students who have been diagnosed with these conditions has grown, so has the number of professionals and educators who are involved in developing effective treatment and educational practices, as well as publishing research on the outcomes of these practices. With this rapid development and expansion, it has become increasingly difficult to assimilate and utilize the varied range of strategies—encompassing behavioral, educational, ancillary or therapeutic, administrative, and family-based interventions. The current book, part of the *Child Clinical Psychology* series, will provide a critical summary of these developments, including an historical review of both the concept of autism as a diagnostic entity, and the lineage of the current best practice methodologies in assessment and intervention. The book utilizes the science of applied behavior analysis as the foundation of the assessment and intervention approach described in the text.

Keywords

applied behavior analysis, autism diagnosis, autism etiology, autism prevalence, autism spectrum disorders, autism, evidence-based practice, functional behavioral assessment, functional daily living skills, function-based treatment

Contents

Acknowledgments

We'd like to thank Peggy Williams and Sam Gontkovsky for their guidance and patience.

To my children who teach and encourage me every day to be mindful, present, and engaged in life. To my husband for always being my supportive teammate. To my mom for her unending support. To my colleagues, family, and friends for their wisdom and conversation. For the children and families with whom I have worked who continue to enlighten me.

—Jessica Glass Kendorski, PhD, NCSP, BCBA-D

To my husband, Dan for his encouragement, patience, and support in this and all my professional endeavors. To my children, Isla and Violet, for their love, patience, and for inspiring me in so many ways. To my friends and family for their love and support. And to all those diagnosed with autism and other intellectual disabilities that I have met and worked with that have taught me so much.

—Amanda Guld Fisher, PhD, BCBA-D

CHAPTER 1

Description and Diagnosis

Autism Spectrum Disorder (ASD) is a diverse neurological disorder that presents during childhood. The complexity of this disorder, spectrum of characteristics and severity, combined with a large amount of unknown information, make for a complicated disorder to diagnose and treat. This chapter will discuss the current accepted diagnostic criteria, history, prevalence, and comorbidity, as well as some of the intricacies involved in this unique disorder.

Diagnosis

Autism Spectrum Disorder (ASD), as it is officially referred in the Diagnostic and Statistical Manual of Mental Disorders-Fifth Edition (DSM 5; American Psychiatric Association [APA], 2013), has long been a disorder that science and society has sought to understand. ASD has an extensive history of varying diagnostic criteria, competing hypotheses of etiology, as well as controversy surrounding effective interventions. This history is likely due to the "spectrum" nature of ASD, where there are very different presentations of behavioral deficits and weaknesses at each end of the spectrum.

The hallmark behavioral presentations of ASD involve deficits in social and emotional communication as well as restricted, repetitive patterns of behavior. The DSM 5 outlines the diagnostic criteria and classification of psychiatric disorders recognized by the U.S. Healthcare System (APA, 2013). According to the DSM 5 diagnostic criteria for ASD, persistent deficits in social and emotional communication across a variety of contexts must be present. These deficits in social and emotional communication include:

1. *Deficits in social and emotional reciprocity.* For a child this may look like difficulty with typical reciprocal conversation, a failure to share emotions and feelings, and a failure to initiate and engage in social

interaction. Specific examples of deficits in social and emotional reciprocity may include: failure to respond to name, failure to show objects to another, lack of shared enjoyment of activities, and talking "at" an individual rather than "to" an individual.

2. *Deficits in nonverbal communication involved in social interaction.* This may present as abnormal eye contact, difficulty with fluent nonverbal communication (e.g., a child may mimic the exact non-vocal communication of another rather than a natural matching of nonvocal responses), or a total lack of facial expressions or gestures to communicate. There may also be a mismatch between the verbal expression of the child and the nonverbal behaviors demonstrated. For example, a child may not show typical joy on face when happy or anger on face when upset.

3. *Deficits in developing and maintaining relationships.* This may look like a lack of interest in engaging with peers, difficulty initiating social interactions, and a lack of shared reciprocal play.

In addition to deficits in social and emotional communication, a child must also present with restricted or repetitive patterns of behavior interests or activities which can include:

1. Repetitive motor movements such as hand flapping and rocking, or repetitive speech such as repeating phrases or lines from videos or television shows.

2. Demonstration of rigid adherence to "sameness" and behavioral difficulty when routines are disrupted.

3. A highly restricted interest in a particular activity, object, or other interest. This is more than just a liking or interest, but rather a perseverative, obsessional focus on an activity or object.

4. Hypo or hypersensitivity to sensory input, specifically, sensitivity to different tactile stimulation on skin or in foods, sensitivity to loud noises, and seeking out different sensory activities such as staring at lights or excessive smelling of things.

These symptoms as outlined in the DSM 5 can vary their presentation in severity on a scale from 1 to 3. Level 1 is defined as requiring support,

Level 2 is defined as requiring substantial support, and Level 3 is defined as requiring very substantial support. In addition to the previously referenced symptomatology, other criteria must be met to diagnose ASD, including, presentation of symptoms in early developmental period (birth to five years), presenting symptoms are not better explained by another diagnosis, and there must be a significant impairment in social, communication, and other areas of adaptive functioning (APA, 2013).

The International Statistical Classification of Diseases and Related Health Problems-10th Revision (ICD-10) is a medical classification by the World Health Organization (WHO, 1992). The ICD-10 outlines diagnostic criteria for disorders similar to ASD, although the disorders are not formerly named ASD. Rather, the ICD-10 classifies Childhood Autism, Atypical Autism, and Asperger Syndrome under the broader classification of Pervasive Developmental Disorders.

Childhood Autism is defined as the presence of impaired development before the age of three years; which includes deficits in three areas of reciprocal social interaction, communication, and restricted, repetitive patterns of behavior. This classification is very similar to the diagnostic criteria outlined in the DSM 5 (APA, 2013; WHO, 1992).

Atypical Autism is defined as atypical development that is present after three years of age, with a lack of impairment in the three areas required for a diagnosis of Childhood Autism. Although the full criteria for Childhood Autism is not met, there is typically a demonstration of deficits in one or two of the areas required for a diagnosis of Childhood Autism such as reciprocal social interaction or communication (WHO, 1992).

An additional "autism-like" classification present in the ICD-10 is Asperger Syndrome. Asperger Syndrome has similar characteristics to Childhood Autism, including deficits in reciprocal social interaction and repetitive stereotyped behaviors; however, a diagnosis of Asperger Syndrome does not require deficits in social communication. This is a major difference from the criteria in the DSM 5, as the most recent revision of the DSM removed the separate classification of Asperger Syndrome. According to DSM 5 criteria, a child presenting with deficits in reciprocal social interaction and repetitive stereotyped behaviors can still meet the criteria of ASD with the presence of typically developing verbal communication skills. This distinction in the United States was not without controversy. Those for the change argue that Asperger Syndrome falls on the spectrum of ASD; however, many families and children identified with Asperger Syndrome are concerned that removing the separate diagnosis may impact clinical service delivery and increase stigmatization (Halfon & Kuo, 2013).

History of Autism Diagnosis

The controversy surrounding Asperger's Syndrome is part of a long history of changes leading to the current accepted diagnostic criteria of ASD. The history of the diagnosis is one where symptomatology necessary to be diagnosed with the disorder varied. Leo Kanner a child psychiatrist in Baltimore, MD was the first to describe what he called "autism" in 1943. He reported seeing children that he described as having a "persistent need for sameness," as well as emotional and social withdrawal. These essential diagnostic features have remained a defining feature of the current diagnosis (Verhoeff, 2013). Throughout the years that followed, the core diagnostic characteristics of autism have changed with each newer edition of the DSM. Originally in DSM I (1952), the features of autism were defined under Childhood Schizophrenic Disorder, likewise, the revision to the DSM II (1968) defined Autistic as a subtype of Schizophrenia. It was not until the third edition of the DSM (1980) that there was the inclusion of "disorders of childhood" which outlined Autistic Disorder as a formal category under Pervasive Developmental Disorders. Finally, with the DSM 5 (2013) there was a renaming of Autistic Disorder to ASD and the current defining diagnostic categories adopted (APA, 2013).

Prevalence and Comorbidity

Since the year 2000, prevalence rates of ASD have been on an increasing trend. According to data from the Center for Disease Control and Prevention (CDC), in the year 2012 about 1 in 68 children have been identified with ASD in the United States. This represents a significant increase in prevalence rates of 1 in 150 in 2000, 1 in 125 in 2004, 1 in 110 in 2006, and 1 in 88 in 2008. Additionally, boys are 4.5 times more likely to be identified than girls, and white children are more likely to be diagnosed than African American and Hispanic children (Christensen et al., 2016). Globally, studies combining North America, Asia, and Europe estimate the prevalence of ASD at about 1 to 2 percent of the total population (APA, 2013). Additional prevalence trends in the United States from 2000 to 2012 indicate that ASD is more prevalent in families of higher socioeconomic status (SES) and in certain areas of the country such as New Jersey (National Academies of Sciences, Engineering, and Medicine, 2015).

The reasons behind the increase in the prevalence of ASD and whether it is still increasing remains a matter of debate. It is unclear if the increase in prevalence can be attributed to an increase in awareness, more specific diagnostic criteria, or a true increase in ASD (APA, 2013). Other factors that may contribute to the increase in prevalence include policies for screening during pediatric well visits, as well as changes in risk factors such as parental age, maternal obesity, and in vitro fertilization; however, these factors alone are unlikely to have contributed to the overall increase in prevalence (National Academies of Sciences, Engineering, and Medicine, 2015).

ASD tends to co-occur with several other disorders, most commonly intellectual disability (i.e., approximately 50 percent of individuals with ASD also have an intellectual disability) as well as various psychiatric disorders including social anxiety disorder, attention deficit hyperactivity disorder, and oppositional defiant disorder (Christensen et al., 2016; Simonoff et al., 2008). Additionally, there are a number of medical concerns that tend to occur in children with ASD, such as sleep disorders, gastrointestinal disorders, feeding disorders, and seizure disorders (Beauchaine & Hinshaw, 2013). Challenging behavior (e.g., aggression, self-injury) is often displayed by children with ASD. This can range from minor challenging behavior to severe behavior disorders. Due to the common presentation of comorbid medical, psychiatric, and behavioral concerns, comprehensive assessment and intervention should include all of these factors.

Early Identification and Diagnosis

Some signs and symptoms of ASD can occur as early as infancy. However, often the signs are not noticed until there becomes a wider developmental gap between the social and communication skills of the child in relation to his or her peers. This delay in diagnosis and intervention can have far-reaching implications. The earlier ASD is diagnosed and intervention is provided, the better social, emotional, and educational outcome for the child (Fernell, Eriksson, & Gillberg, 2013). The American Academy of Pediatrics (AAP) recommends that pediatricians screen children for ASD at 9, 18, and 24 and/or 30 months of age, and children with a positive screen receive a comprehensive evaluation (2016).

Recent research has identified some early behavioral signs of ASD to help aid in identification and intervention. One particular longitudinal study examined children at 6, 12, 18, 24, and 36 months of age. The findings indicated that at age 6 months, there were no real differences between children typically developing and those who later developed ASD; however, during the next 12 months those children eventually diagnosed with ASD demonstrated loss of skills, and declining social communication behavior (i.e., gaze to faces, shared smiles, and vocalizations; Ozonoff et al., 2010). In sum, these findings support the idea that there are symptoms of ASD as early as 12 months of age, and underscore the need for continued research into earlier behavioral markers that can aid in the identification of ASD.

A recurring theme in the research of ASD and public awareness campaigns is the concept of *early intervention*. In the United States as of 2012 the median age for a comprehensive evaluation was 40 months, with only approximately 43 percent of children receiving a comprehensive evaluation by 36 months. Additionally, most children in the United States were diagnosed at four years of age, two years after ASD can be reliably diagnosed (Christensen et al., 2016). To help support earlier identification, the CDC launched the *Learn the Signs. Act Early* public awareness campaign as well. *Healthy People 2020* aimed to identify and evaluate at least 47 percent of children with ASD before 36 months. Research continues to support the effectiveness of early intensive intervention for children with ASD to the level that children are often found to be indistinguishable from same age peers after a few years of early intensive (25 to 40 hours per week) behavioral intervention (e.g., Lovaas, 1987; Jacobson, Mulick, & Green, 1998; Smith Eikeseth, Klevstrand & Lovaas, 1997; Smith & Lovaas, 1998; McEachin, Smith, & Lovaas, 1993).

Typical Development and Early Signs of ASD

The American Academy of Pediatrics recommends that all children are monitored and screened on their developmental milestones between the ages of birth to five years (Council on Children with Disabilities, 2006). The U.S. Department of Health and Human Services *Birth to 5: Watch Me Thrive* initiative is aimed at promoting behavioral and developmental screenings to assess language, social, and motor development, in an effort to identify and intervene early. Understanding typical developmental milestones can aid parents and caregivers in identifying the signs of ASD.

Often, children with ASD may demonstrate early signs of social differences that become more pronounced as they further develop. These differences can include a lack of eye contact, failure to respond to his or her name, failure to point and look at others while pointing, a lack of imitation, and a lack of appropriate facial expressions. A child with some of these characteristics may be described by parents as a "good baby" since the child may not necessarily seek out the parent for social interaction. Children with typical social development will spontaneously seek out the parent and want to share objects, items, and emotional experiences, known as shared enjoyment. This is often absent in a child showing signs of ASD.

There are also marked communication differences between a child developing typically and a child with ASD. Noticed first, is often a delay in receptive and expressive language development, specifically, not stating single words by 16 months of age, a lack of nonverbal communication such as gesturing or pointing, and not responding to the communication of others. At times, parents may report that their child is having hearing difficulty due to the child's lack of response. In addition to delays in expressive and receptive language, there is likely a lack of initiation of communication, as well as reciprocal (back and forth) communication. For example, a child as young as 6 months will be able to communicate that they need help, by actively trying to get the parent's attention through looking at the parent's face, crying, and attempting to engage the parent. However, a child showing signs of ASD may not initiate that they need help, instead the child may cry to themselves or use their parents hand as a "tool" to get what they need, rather than communicate *with* parent.

Finally, children showing early signs of ASD may show behavioral deficits and excesses, (i.e., too little or too much of a behavior) expected for a child developing typically. Most notably a child may show self-stimulatory behavior which can include rocking, flapping hands, or cupping ears. Additionally, children with ASD may be hypersensitive to various noises, textures on clothing, and lights. A persistence for routines and rituals and an obsession over a particular item or activity may also be present. Children developing typically may at certain developmental periods show a desire for sameness, such as reading the same book over and over, but this will be much more pronounced in a child with early ASD.

Prevalence and Representation in Special Education

While ASD is a psychiatric and medical diagnosis, autism is also a classification under Individuals with Disabilities Education Act (IDEA; Public Law 108–446) for eligibility for Special Education. IDEA is a federal law requiring schools to provide services to children with disabilities that impede educational performance and are found eligible for special education services. Autism is one of the classifications under IDEA for eligibility for special education and is defined as:

i. Autism means a developmental disability significantly affecting verbal and nonverbal communication and social interaction, generally evident before age three, that adversely affects a child's educational performance. Other characteristics often associated with autism are engagement in repetitive activities and stereotyped movements, resistance to environmental change or change in daily routines, and unusual responses to sensory experiences.

ii. Autism does not apply if a child's educational performance is adversely affected primarily because the child has an emotional disturbance, as defined in paragraph (c)(4) of this section.

iii. A child who manifests the characteristics of autism after age three could be identified as having autism if the criteria in paragraph (c)(1) (i) of this section are satisfied *[34 C.F.R. 300.8 (c) (i)(ii) (ii)]*.

Much of the defining characteristics of autism under IDEA are similar to the diagnostic criteria outlined in the DSM-5, including deficits in social interaction, and presence of stereotyped behavior. The major requirement of IDEA classification mandates that symptoms "adversely affects educational performance." Since IDEA classification is for the provision of individual education services, any classification would require a negative impact in educational performance. Specifics of assessment for classification are outlined later in Chapter 3.

Prevalence data by the U.S. Department of Education, National Center for Education Statistics (2016), reveal that in 2012 to 2013 there were approximately 498,000 students receiving special education services under the classification of autism. Additionally, 1 percent of total students enrolled in Pre-Kindergarten through 12th grade were receiving special education services under the classification of autism. Additional analysis of prevalence has shown a significant increase. In 1992, 15,556 children (6 to 22 years) were classified with autism, by 2011 this number has increased "25 fold" (National Academies Press, 2015).

Behavior Analytic Approach to this Book

A functional approach to assess the behavioral symptomatology and physiological concerns with the goal of developing evidence-based intervention is essential to the treatment of ASD. As such, the framework of this book will focus on a functional approach to assessment and treatment. The assessment and interventions outlined in remaining chapters will be addressed from an applied behavior analytic framework, specifically, focusing on assessment and analysis that leads to evidenced-based interventions to identify strengths, improve functional deficits, and promote skill acquisition. Applied behavior analysis is the science of changing socially significant behaviors using proven behavioral principles, while demonstrating effectiveness through systematic application and analysis. For an in depth discussion of the field of applied behavior analysis, please see the textbook entitled *Applied Behavior Analysis* (Cooper, Heward, & Heron, 2007).

Consistent with a commitment to evidence-based assessment and interventions, the chapters herein will not include any interventions without empirical support. While this book is not an exhaustive overview of all evidence-based interventions, attention was paid to include interventions with strong empirical support that are widely used. As such, his book will include evidence-based assessment and intervention strategies that meet many or all of the seven dimensions of Applied Behavior Analysis (Baer, Wolf, & Risley, 1968):

Applied—assessments and interventions included will be related to problems of social importance.

Behavioral—assessments and interventions will focus on measurable, observable behavior that can be directly observed.

Analytic—programming will focus on assessing the effectiveness of interventions and interventions presented will have demonstrated research support.

Technological—interventions will be objectively defined in enough detail so that they can be implemented by parents, caregivers, teachers, instructional aides, school psychologists, behavior analysts, and other professionals.

Conceptually Systematic—assessments and interventions will be grounded in behavioral theory.

Effective—interventions presented will produce clinically significant changes in behavior and meaningful benefits to the individual's quality of life.

Generality—interventions can be generalized across people, environments, responses, and time. Strategies for programming generalization will be discussed.

CHAPTER 2

Conceptualization

Etiology

Currently, extensive research from varying scientific disciplines is being conducted on the causes of Autism Spectrum Disorder (ASD). While evidence for a single cause to ASD is lacking, a combination of genetic, biological, and environmental influences have been implicated. Namely, certain risk factors have been identified through their frequency of co-occurrence with ASD. It should be noted that the majority of the research is correlational, that is, these factors tend to co-occur with ASD, but a causal relationship between the two has not been found. Additionally, which specific genetic, biological, and environmental influences increase the risk of ASD and in which combination is not yet known (Grafodatskaya et al., 2010).

Neurodevelopmental Hypothesis

Identifying a single biological or environmental determinant of ASD is unlikely, as the etiology is likely due to the reciprocal effects of the complex interaction of biological and environmental variables. Advances in technology have shed light on possible disruptions in fetal nervous system development and the manifestation of symptoms in childhood and later adolescence. (Trottier, Srivastava, & Walker, 1999). The notion that certain disorders have their origins in prenatal and infant impairment of the brain and central nervous system is known as the neurodevelopmental hypothesis. The neurodevelopmental hypothesis posits that disruptions to the developing brain and central nervous system during critical developmental periods such as the first and second trimester present risk factors for the development of disorders of early childhood, and even adolescence and late adulthood. Specific pregnancy and birth risks include lack of oxygen at birth, thalidomide poisoning, congenital rubella, encephalitis, measles, and mumps (Chess, Korn, & Fernandez, 1971; Trottier et al., 1999).

Genetic Influences

Since the causes of ASD are likely a combination of genetic and environmental factors, there has been a significant increase in research to identify the role that genes play in the development of ASD (Grafodatskaya et al., 2010). These findings on genetic determinants include:

- There is an increased risk of being diagnosed with ASD if the child has a sibling with a diagnosis of ASD (Bailey, Phillips, & Rutter, 1996; Szatmari et al., 1993).
- ASD tends to co-occur with a number of other genetic conditions including Rett, Fragile X, Prader-Willi, Angelman, and CHARGE (Grafodatskaya et al., 2010).
- Certain genes, specifically the duplication of 15q11–13 has been identified in 1 to 2 percent of ASD cases and risk is estimated at more than 85 percent in individuals with this duplication (Grafodatskaya et al., 2010).

Additionally, certain environmental factors have been studied to determine if they lead to changes in epigenetic marks (turning on and turning off of gene expressions), which can lead to an increased risk of ASD. One identified environmental exposure that influences gene expression is prenatal exposure to valproate, an antiseizure drug commonly used to treat seizure disorder, bipolar disorder, and migraine headaches (Roullet, Lai, & Foster, 2013; Grafodatskaya et al., 2010). Similarly, studies have been conducted on the effects of pesticide exposure and ASD symptoms. While the mechanisms for which pesticides could potentially affect the developing fetus are scientifically understood, the research is not yet conclusive on whether pesticides actually increase ASD risk and how (Shelton, Hertz-Piccioto, & Pessah, 2012). These relationships are only two hypotheses of how environmental influences and biological factors interact, particularly at the genetic level, to potentially increase the risk of ASD symptomatology; many more may develop over time.

Environmental Risk Factors

A number of perinatal and neonatal factors have been associated with an increased risk of ASD (Gardner, Spiegelman, & Buka, 2011). Many of these factors were identified through a meta-analysis, which involves reviewing the research evidence from individual published studies and combining these findings to compile a list of specific risk factors. Perinatal factors are those that occur in the few weeks immediately before and immediately following birth; whereas postnatal factors are those that occur in the time following birth. The identification of perinatal and postnatal factors contributing to an increased risk of ASD supports the neuro-developmental hypothesis of ASD. Specifically, there is a critical period for developing ASD that occurs before birth, during the birthing process, and immediately following birth (Gardner, Spiegelman, & Buka, 2011). However, it should be noted that these factors have only been identified as having an association with an increased risk, but a 1:1 correspondence has not been found.

Factors that occur perinatally, immediately prior, during, and following birth associated with an increased risk of ASD include: abnormal presentation during delivery, including breech position of the infant, as well as umbilical cord complications, such as a prolapsed cord or a cord wrapped around the neck of the infant. Additional factors include fetal distress, trauma during birth, multiple births, maternal hemorrhage, and abnormally high or low birth weight. A low 5-minute Apgar score, meconium aspiration, feeding difficulties, anemia, Rh factor incompatibility, and hyperbilirubinemia were also implicated as contributing to increased risk. Prenatal factors associated with increased risk include: advanced paternal and maternal age at birth, maternal gestational bleeding, gestational diabetes, being first born, and maternal prenatal medication (Gardner, Spiegelman, & Buka, 2009). Metabolic conditions, specifically diabetes, hypertension, and obesity have been associated with an increased risk in developmental delays (Krakowiak et al., 2012). Early analysis of the commonalities of these risk factors suggests a couple of hypotheses. The first, many of these risk factors such as trauma during birth, cord complications, and abnormal presentation could be the result of decreased oxygen deprivation at birth or hypoxia (Gardner et al., 2009). Additionally, giving birth in the summer months as well as maternal fever is correlated with increased risk of ASD and could suggest a potential maternal infection during the winter months of the first and second trimester; specifically, conception during the months of December, January, February, and March (Gardner et al., 2009; Zerbo et al., 2011, 2013).

While this early research provides some insight into the multiple factors that may be associated with ASD, it is important to not overstate the findings. Each factor correlated with ASD could be the result of a combination of factors and the exact causal mechanisms are only hypotheses at this point. Researchers are still in the very beginning stages of researching the etiology of ASD. As Gardner and his colleagues (2009) point out "the perinatal and neonatal complications identified in the current analysis may be the result of previous prenatal complications and/or may operate in combination with prior prenatal complications to impact autism risk" (p. 349).

Factors Ruled Out as Risk Factors

While research leading to the identification of environmental and biological risk factors is essential, of equal importance is the identification of factors that do not contribute to increased risk. Perhaps the most studied, most feared, and most misunderstood are vaccinations, particularly the measles, mumps, and rubella (MMR) vaccines. Multiple studies involving thousands of children with ASD have been conducted and have found no relationship between vaccinations and increased risk for ASD. A recent meta-analysis conducted on case control and cohort studies revealed no relationship between vaccinations and ASD, no relationship between the MMR vaccination and ASD, and no relationship between mercury and thimerasol and ASD (Taylor, Swerdfeger, & Eslick, 2014). In fact, only one study showed a link between the MMR vaccine and ASD; however, due to unethical and unscientific study design the journal retracted the publication and subsequently the author lost his medical license (The

Editors of the Lancet, 2010). Additionally, a study conducted on the effects vaccinations have on the body, specifically increasing antibody stimulation proteins and polysaccharides was not shown to increase the risk of ASD (DeStefano, Price, & Weintraub, 2013).

Protective Factors

As of now, the best protective factors are those that provide for healthy prenatal development including nutrition, limiting teratogens, as well as promoting a safe delivery (Gardner et al., 2009). Behaviorally, early identification and intervention is the number one protective factor toward minimizing the impact of ASD on a child's social, emotional, cognitive, and behavioral development. The earlier ASD is identified and evidence-based interventions (EBIs) are initiated, the better the outcome.

Evidence-Based Interventions

Federal legislation outlined in the Individuals with Disabilities Education Act (IDEA) specifies the requirement of the use of EBIs in schools. While EBIs are not specifically defined in IDEA, there is professional agreement that EBIs are interventions that are scientifically validated for effectiveness in a sufficient number of well-designed research studies. EBIs rely on data collection and outcomes to determine their effectiveness for the goals identified. The importance of EBIs is to ensure that treatment provided to a child diagnosed with ASD is effective, as well as limit the use of ineffective treatments or discontinue ineffective treatments quickly. Avoiding ineffective (especially fad and pseudoscientific) interventions will help to minimize wasting money, time, and other resources, as well as avoid potential risk of injury to the child (Newell, 2006).

Professional organizations and research synthesis organizations have helped compile a list of EBIs for all children including children diagnosed with ASD. The U.S. Department of Education has developed the What Works Clearinghouse (WWC) to evaluate scientific studies on intervention effectiveness. This organization consists of certified reviewers who review research in education and determine if the results meet the specified requirements for effective interventions. The WWC rates intervention studies according to sound scientific criteria consisting of the following: random assignment of the groups studied, the similarities of the groups compared, study design, and analysis of confounding variables. The interventions are then rated as meeting the standards of the WWC, meeting the standards with reservations, and not meeting standards (http://ies.ed.gov/ncee/wwc/FWW). Additionally, the National Autism Center (NAC) developed Evidence-Based Practice and Autism in the schools—2nd Edition which compiles lists of EBI's rated according to similar criteria (NAC, 2015). Similarly, the American Psychological Association Society for Clinical Psychology (Division 12) formed a presidential task force to disseminate evidence-based practice for treatment of psychological disorders (American Psychological Association, 2006). Many of the interventions discussed later in this book will come from some of these sources. With intervention in mind, let's explore assessment in ASD.

CHAPTER 3

Evaluation and Assessment

What Is the Process of ASD Assessment?

Developmental Surveillance

The American Academy of Pediatrics (AAP, 2016) recommends developmental surveillance for all children to ensure that developmental problems are identified early. The AAP recommends surveillance at *every* well child visit which includes: soliciting feedback from primary caregivers on developmental milestones, maintaining a developmental history, observations of the child during the visit, and identification of risk and protective factors. In addition to developmental surveillance, a more targeted screening of children to look for specific behavioral symptoms related to ASD and other developmental disabilities is also recommended.

Screening

Early screening of infants and children is the essential first step in the identification of ASD. Early identification of ASD is crucial to the initiation of evidence-based interventions and support for the child and family. The American Academy of Child & Adolescent Psychiatry (AACP) and the AAP recommend the developmental assessment of all children which includes a measure of ASD symptomatology (Volkmar et al., 2014; Johnson & Myers, 2007). The AAP recommends that all children be screened with a standardized developmental tool at 9, 18, and 24 or 30 months of age. Additional screening assessments should be conducted at other times if the parent expresses concern, the pediatrician notices a concern (such as lack of responding to name, lack of eye contact, or delayed speech), or the child has additional risk factors such as having a sibling with ASD

(Johnson & Myers, 2007). The parent combined with the pediatrician is typically the first to identify developmental delays and possible ASD symptoms. Even if a child does not present primary symptoms at developmental screens, there should still be monitoring of developmental milestones during pediatric visits.

Screening Instruments

With respect to screening instruments, the effectiveness ultimately depends on their sensitivity and specificity. Sensitivity is the degree to which the screening instrument can correctly identify an individual with the disorder. Specificity refers to correctly identifying children who do have the disorder. Sensitivity is often referred to as having an accurate rate of "true positives," as in when a child is screened positive for ASD, and ultimately does have ASD. Specificity is referred to as having an appropriate degree of "true negatives," as in when a child is screened negative for ASD, and ultimately does not have ASD. Screening tools strive to have adequate sensitivity and specificity; however, greater sensitivity is often of more importance as it is preferable to ensure that a child with ASD is not missed.

While there are a great number of screening tools, they have fundamental differences in who completes the screen (parent vs. practitioner), and if the screening tool assesses typical development only, or includes ASD specific symptomatology. A common screener for children younger than 18 months is the *Infant/Toddler Checklist* from the Communication and Symbolic Behavior Scales Developmental Profile, which has a specific focus on social and communication skills, and was found to have strong predictive validity in identification of ASD (Wetherby, 2003; Pierce et al., 2011). The *Modified Checklist for Autism in Toddlers*, Revised is a screen developed for children 16 to 30 months of age and is designed specifically to screen for the presence or absence of behaviors related to ASD (Robins et al., 2014). The *Screening Tool for Autism* differs from the others listed in that it is an interactive screener designed for use with educational practitioners to screen for ASD symptomatology in children between 24 and 36 months of ages (Stone, Coonrod, Turner, & Pozdol, 2004).

How Is ASD Diagnosed?

Diagnostic Assessment

If a screening is negative for ASD, then no further diagnostic testing is necessary; however, continued surveillance of development is recommended. If screening is positive for behavioral symptoms of ASD then additional diagnostic assessment should be performed. Please see Figure 3.1 for an overview of the process of screening and diagnosis. The diagnostic assessment process should consist of a review of relevant background information and family history, a physical examination, and a developmental or psychometric evaluation to determine if behavioral symptomatology meets the criteria for ASD (Johnson & Myers, 2007). Diagnostic assessment should also include assessment of other related psychiatric and medical diagnoses to either rule out a diagnosis of ASD or confirm a possible comorbid diagnosis (Volkmar et al., 2014).

Diagnostic Instruments

While screening instruments can be likened to taking someone's temperature to confirm whether or not they may be sick, diagnostic assessments are more comprehensive and help to get to the root cause of the symptoms or to classify a group of symptoms for treatment or intervention.

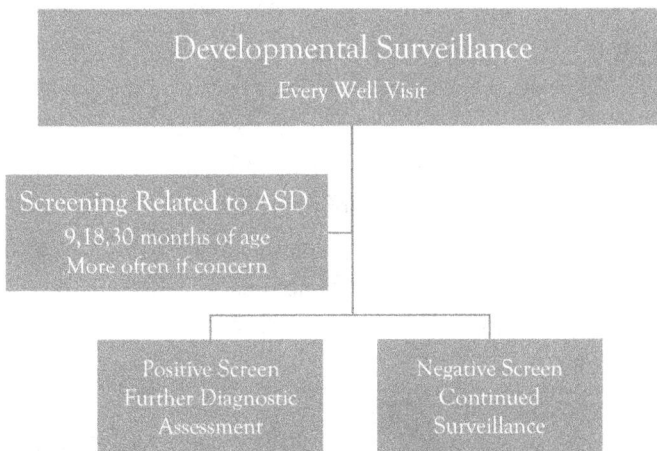

Figure 3.1 This diagram depicts the relationship of screening and diagnostic assessment for children

Screening identifies that there may be a developmental concern, but diagnostic assessment helps determine what else may be of issue and what may be the cause of the concern. The first step in any diagnostic assessment is a comprehensive physical evaluation to rule out any medical concerns that may account for any presenting symptoms. If other medical reasons are ruled out as causing the symptoms, then additional diagnostic testing should be initiated.

Specific diagnostic testing related to ASD can include parent or caregiver interviews that are rated by clinicians, as well as task-based standardized assessments. Most interviews and task-based assessments are standardized and norm-referenced to determine if the ratings and performance are similar to those meeting the criteria for ASD according to the DSM 5 (APA, 2013). The AACAP identifies three widely used diagnostic instruments (although there are others), including the Autism Diagnostic Interview, Revised (ADI-R), the Diagnostic Interview for Social and Communication Disorders (DISCO), and the Autism Diagnostic Observation Schedule (ADOS).

Both the ADI-R and the DISCO are parent or caregiver interviews that are rated by a clinician. The ADI-R is for use with children with a cognitive age of 2 years or above and assesses relevant domains related to ASD including: Language Communication, Reciprocal Social Interaction, and Repetitive Behaviors or Interests (Rutter & LeCouteur, 2003). The DISCO is a semistructured interview designed to collect information on developmental skills, and identify impairments related to ASD such as social communication, repetitive behaviors, as well as potential comorbid diagnoses (Wing et al., 2002). Both tools can be used to collect a wide amount of information on various behaviors that may meet the criteria for ASD.

The ADOS differs from the ADI-R and the DISCO in that it is a standardized behavior observation of the child in relation to individuals and the environment. The ADOS is published by Western Psychological Services, and is designed to assess symptoms of ASD from ages of 12 months through adulthood. Specific behaviors assessed are closely aligned to behavioral aspects of ASD, such as reciprocal interaction with caregivers and clinicians, pretend play, joint attention and enjoyment, and perspective taking. The ADOS is considered a crucial assessment in the diagnosis of ASD due to the direct observation of contrived situations that will determine if symptoms of ASD exist. The direct observation can be considered more accurate and reliable than subjective ratings and reports by caregivers. The clinician will set up different activities designed to evoke social and communicative behaviors and then score each observation according to standardized criteria, which are then compared to normative cutoff skills for ASD symptomatology.

Sensory Assessment

An important defining feature in ASD is sensory difficulties classified in the DSM 5 (APA, 2013) under "restricted, repetitive patterns of behavior, interest, or activities" (p. 50). Sensory difficulties present in ASD include hypo-reactivity, characterized by a diminished response or awareness of environmental stimuli; hyper-reactivity, characterized by an overactive response to environmental stimuli; unusual sensory behaviors, characterized by sensation-seeking or sensation-avoiding; and unusual sensory perception, characterized by abnormal organization and interpretation of sensory stimuli in the environment (Schaaf & Lane, 2015). While many of the instruments designed to aid in the diagnosis of ASD include some aspects of sensory assessment, they do not provide an exclusive comprehensive evaluation of sensory concerns. Given the significance of sensory concerns in children with ASD, a comprehensive assessment of sensory features based on parental report and direct observation is recommended (Schaaf & Lane, 2015). This type of assessment may need to be individualized, and can aid in the diagnosis of ASD as well as establish specific goals for intervention.

What Distinguishes ASD from Other Disorders?

ASD has similar diagnostic criteria to other disorders, and a comprehensive assessment involves ruling out or confirming other similar diagnoses. In younger children ASD can mimic symptoms of Rett Syndrome, Selective Mutism, Language disorders including Social (Pragmatic) Communication Disorder, Intellectual Disability without ASD, Stereotypic Movement Disorder, Attention-Deficit Hyperactivity Disorder (ADHD), and Schizophrenia (APA, 2013). Additionally, in older children ASD can mimic the symptoms of Social Anxiety Disorder and Generalized Anxiety Disorder. The following is a table of shared characteristics and symptoms that may better fit the criteria of ASD and differentiate from other disorders, based on DSM 5 (APA, 2013, p. 57–58).

Diagnosis	Shared characteristics and differences from ASD
Rett Disorder	During the regression phase, children (girls) may show difficulty in social interaction skills; however, in later stages communication and social interaction will likely return or improve.
Selective Mutism	While there is a lack of social communication in Selective Mutism, there are often intact social reciprocity skills.
Social (Pragmatic) Disorder	In Social (Pragmatic) Disorder there is language impairment that may impact social communication skills, but generally there is the absence of repetitive, stereotyped behavior.
Intellectual Disability without ASD	In Intellectual Disability with ASD there is typically a discrepancy between social functioning and other nonverbal skills. If there is not a discrepancy between social communication and other developmental skills, then the criteria for ASD are not met.
Stereotypic Movement Disorder	As identified by the DSM 5, stereotyped movements are a feature of ASD so Stereotypic Movement Disorder is not an added diagnosis. However, if an individual with ASD has stereotypic movement that causes injury or is the primary focus of treatment, it may warrant this diagnosis.
ADHD	Attention difficulties are often present in children with ASD; however, an additional diagnosis of ADHD is not included unless the attentional difficulties or hyperactivity exceed that of "comparable mental age." Children with just ADHD may show better skills in social connection than children with ASD.
Schizophrenia	Hallucinations and delusions are not present in ASD.

American Psychiatric Association, (2013)

Assessment Interpretation and Diagnosis

Following the collection of relevant data through a variety of assessments, the results should be pulled together to determine if the child's symptoms are consistent with ASD. Since ASD is a complex diagnosis involving a variety of behavioral, social, psychological, and medical symptoms, the interpretation and final diagnosis should be conducted in a multi-disciplinary fashion including a team of relevant professionals (Volkmar et al., 2014). A comprehensive assessment would involve incorporating the assessments from relevant disciplines (e.g., speech therapy, psychology, medicine, occupational therapy) to obtain a full picture of the child's current functioning. All assessment data should be compared to the criteria outlined in the DSM 5 (APA, 2013) to determine if the criteria for ASD are met. Assessment data from multiple disciplines are also crucial to developing specific goals and interventions in the areas identified.

How Is ASD Classified in the School Environment?

Diagnosis Versus Classification in Schools

The primary purpose for a diagnosis of any kind is to aid in treatment and intervention. Often, a diagnosis of ASD provides the opportunity for funding of services in the preschool, school, and home environment. Assessment and intervention for children with any type of developmental delay is a mandate of the Individuals with Disabilities Education Act (IDEA; Public Law 108 to 446) and thus provides access to vital services provided within the school setting.

Early Intervention IDEA-Part C

Early Intervention services are a federal mandate for children birth to 3 years that have demonstrated a need outlined in Part C of IDEA. This federal mandate outlines the minimum requirements that individual states must follow regarding Early Intervention. IDEA specifies that states must make efforts to identify children experiencing a developmental delay and provide appropriate assessment in cognitive, communication, social and emotional, physical, and adaptive development; or if a child has a diagnosed physical or mental condition that is likely to result in a developmental delay. Additionally, the law specifies that interventions should be provided in the child's natural environment to the "maximum extent possible." While different states will have different laws related to early intervention and school-related services, the mandate also allows for the extension of early intervention services until a child begins Kindergarten (U.S. Department of Education, 2016).

Autism Classification for School-Age Children

Conceivably a diagnosis of ASD by a medical professional or other qualified professional will often lead to a classification of autism to qualify for Special Education Services; however, this is not always the case. Federal

Law requires that determination for eligibility be made by a multidisciplinary team which can consist of parents, clinicians, general and special education teachers, speech, occupational, and physical therapists (Klose et al., 2012). Often a comprehensive evaluation is performed and the need for special education services and subsequent classification is determined. Perhaps the most important aspect in determining an autism classification for special education surrounds level of impairment. The team must make a decision that the child's impairment reaches the level that it negatively impacts performance in the educational environment. Therefore, a multidisciplinary classification is the necessary and sufficient component of a classification. An autism diagnosis by a licensed professional is often needed but not always sufficient for special education services.

A diagnostic assessment is often required in order to fund services in the school or home setting. However, diagnostic assessments do not always aid in the development of the specific interventions used in these settings. The following sections are specific assessments needed to develop interventions to address and minimize the specific characteristics of ASD that are identified during the diagnosis. These assessments are typically conducted by the clinicians designing and implementing the specific interventions as members of the multidisciplinary teams. The assessments are used first to design interventions in a variety of areas and then to monitor the effectiveness of the interventions once implemented.

Functional Behavioral Assessments

A functional behavioral assessment (FBA) is a method of determining the relationship between specific environmental variables and behavior. Often FBAs are initiated to help reduce a "problem" behavior and increase appropriate behavior in the home, school, and community. For example, suppose a child with ASD begins to scream after he is asked to get dressed for school. The parent indicates that the child appears to engage in this behavior for "no reason." An FBA will help determine *why* the child is engaging in the behavior, such as to avoid getting dressed for school, to continue to engage in the activity he was performing before being asked to get dressed, or possibly to access or escape parent attention.

Once the *why* of the behavior is determined, then the development of a function-based intervention, based on evidence from published research, can be developed.

It is important to note that a "problem" behavior is most likely a problem for the individuals around the child (parent, teacher, peers) but is likely not a problem for the child. More specifically, while the behavior may not be preferred or desired by those around them, it is likely serving a purpose (function) for the child. Figuring out the function of the behavior and subsequent adaptive replacements is the goal of the functional behavioral assessment.

How Is an FBA Different from Other Assessments?

An FBA is different from other types of evaluations in that the assessor is using the most objective methods possible to collect data on environmental events that affect an observable behavior. The logic of an FBA is based on several assumptions. These assumptions include that behavior is learned and serves some environmental function and that behavior continues because it serves some function, or is reinforced. People (children with ASD included) rarely continue to engage in some behavior if it does not result in reinforcement.

What Is Reinforcement?

In order to understand the common functions of behavior, it is important to understand the principle of reinforcement. In short, behavior that is reinforced, continues. Reinforcement can come in many forms and is defined functionally (i.e., based on how it affects behavior). That is, reinforcement is said to occur when a change in the environment that follows behavior (i.e., a consequence) results in that behavior being repeated again in the future. Reinforcement can also be social or automatic. Social reinforcement is reinforcement that is delivered by another person, and automatic reinforcement is reinforcement that is a direct result of the behavior itself. For example, assume that being in a well-lit room is reinforcing. A person can engage in different types of behavior that result in a well-lit room, such as asking another person to turn on the light. In this example, the behavior is a request (e.g., "Can you turn on the light, please?") and the reinforcer is another person flipping a light switch. We would call this socially mediated (or socially delivered) reinforcement. Alternatively, a person can individually flip a light switch. This behavior (i.e., flipping the light switch for yourself) results in the same reinforcer (i.e., a well-lit room) without any other person intervening. The reinforcement in this example would be called automatic reinforcement, since the reinforcement is a direct result of the behavior without any other person needed to deliver it.

The change in the environment with reinforcement can involve something being added to the environment or removed from the environment. When a reinforcer involves a stimulus added to the environment, it is said to be a positive reinforcer. When a reinforcer involves a stimulus removed from the environment, it is said to be a negative reinforcer. For example, when a child screams in the checkout line of a grocery store because in the past, she has received candy and therefore, will continue to do so in the future; this is an example of positive reinforcement. The child's behavior resulted in obtaining the candy. Alternatively, when a child screams during dinner because in the past that has resulted in her not having to finish her vegetables, and she is more likely to do this in the future; this is an example of negative reinforcement. The child's behavior resulted in the removal of the vegetables. This relationship between behavior and environmental variables is referred to as the behavioral function.

Functional result	Stimulus added to the environment	Stimulus removed from the environment
Behavior increases	Positive reinforcement	Negative reinforcement
Behavior decreases	Positive punishment	Negative punishment

What Are the Functions of Behavior?

Most behavior (including problem or challenging behavior) functions to access (positive reinforcement) or escape (negative reinforcement) something. Therefore, there are often said to be four main functions of behavior. Behavior can function to obtain positive social reinforcement, negative social reinforcement, positive automatic reinforcement, or

```
                        ┌─────────────┐
                        │  Behavioral │
                        │  Function   │
                        └─────────────┘
                    ┌───────────┴───────────┐
              ┌──────────┐            ┌──────────┐
              │  Access  │            │  Escape  │
              └──────────┘            └──────────┘
          ┌───────┴───────┐        ┌───────┴───────┐
  ┌───────────┐  ┌───────────┐  ┌───────────┐  ┌───────────┐
  │  Social   │  │ Automatic │  │  Social   │  │ Automatic │
  │Reinforcement│ │Reinforcement│ │Reinforcement│ │Reinforcement│
  └───────────┘  └───────────┘  └───────────┘  └───────────┘
```

Social Positive Reinforcement	Automatic Positive Reinforcement	Social Negative Reinforcement	Automatic Negative Reinforcement
Examples: Access to toys, praise, reprimands, food, etc.	Examples: Access to sound, noise, light, taste, etc.	Examples: Escape from tasks, social situations, etc.	Examples: Escape from pain, itch, touch, etc.

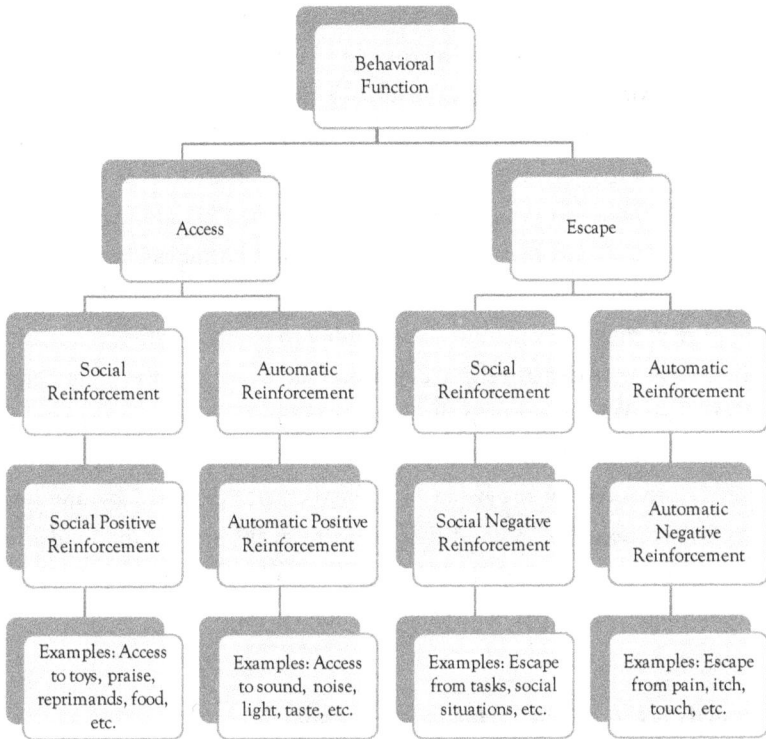

Figure 3.2 This figure depicts the common functions of behavior

negative automatic reinforcement. Figure 3.2 outlines the functions and their effect on behavior.

A behavior that functions to obtain positive social reinforcement is a behavior that in the past has resulted in another individual delivering some change in the environment that involves the addition of some stimulus. The previous example of a child screaming in the grocery store to get candy, is an example of positive social reinforcement because the candy is a stimulus added (positive) to the environment, and it is delivered by another person (social). Whereas a behavior that has a negative social reinforcement function is one that in the past has resulted in another individual removing an aversive stimulus (a stimulus from which an individual will escape) from the situation. The previous example of a child screaming to have his plate of vegetables removed is an example of negative social reinforcement because the vegetables were removed (negative) from the environment by another person (social).

A behavior that functions to obtain positive automatic reinforcement is a behavior that in the past has resulted in some change in the environment that involves the addition of some stimulus that is directly produced by the behavior itself (i.e., not delivered by another person). For example, a child that screams in a quiet and boring environment in order to produce an exciting sound, and then screams to get this sound in future boring environments, is screaming to obtain positive automatic reinforcement. Alternatively, a behavior that has a negative automatic function is a behavior that in the past has resulted in some change in the environment that involves the removal of some aversive stimulus that is directly produced by the behavior itself (i.e., not delivered by another person). For example, a child that hums to avoid hearing the loud fire siren, and in the future continues to hum when in the presence of a siren, is humming maintained by negative reinforcement.

What Is a Functional Behavioral Assessment?

The term Functional Behavioral Assessment (FBA) refers to the process of gathering information about the environmental events that predict and maintain a target behavior. An FBA involves a variety of methods that vary in their precision and complexity. The three main methods of an FBA are indirect assessment, direct (also called descriptive) assessment, and functional analysis (also known as FA or systematic manipulation). A functional behavioral assessment should always include more than one method and should always include at least one direct assessment method. The more complex and precise methods should be used with more complex behavior situations such as more severe challenging behavior, long-standing behavior problems, and other complex situations (O'Neill et al., 2015).

Why Conduct a Functional Behavioral Assessment?

The main reason for conducting an FBA is to enable conceptualization of a more effective and individualized intervention plan. Research has shown that interventions based on the results of FBAs are more effective than interventions selected based on other factors such as clinician preference (Newcomer & Lewis, 2004; Ingram, Lewis-Palmer, & Sugai, 2005). In addition, there have been several recent regulations at the state and federal level that support that a functional behavioral assessment is best practice in developing effective intervention plans (e.g., Individuals with Disabilities Education Act). FBAs are also described as best practice in the ethical codes of many professions, such as the Behavior Analyst Certification Board, American Psychological Association, and the National Association of School Psychologists.

When Should an FBA Be Conducted?

Several specific legislations dictate in what circumstances an FBA should be conducted. For example, IDEA, originally enacted as P.L. 94-142, specifies that FBAs should be conducted no later than after 10 days of suspension for problem behavior and before a change to a more restrictive educational placement (20 USC §1400 et seq). Professional ethical codes also describe when FBAs should be conducted. For example, the Guidelines for Responsible Conduct for Behavior Analysts (3.02 Functional Behavioral Assessment) state that behavior analysts should conduct an FBA prior to implementing a behavior plan to decrease a challenging behavior. This is often considered best practice as it is based on the research that conducting an FBA prior to selecting a treatment will result in better and more efficient outcomes (Newcomer & Lewis, 2004; Ingram, Lewis-Palmer, & Sugai, 2005).

Where Is an FBA Conducted?

Indirect assessments, which typically involve interviewing or surveying those who have knowledge of the target behavior, can be conducted in the most convenient areas and times for the caregivers (e.g., homes, classrooms). However, sometimes parents and caregivers may give more accurate information if they are asked about the behavior in quiet, less-distracting settings, and possibly even in the settings where the target behavior often occurs (to assist in memory).

Direct assessments, which include attempts at direct observation of the behavior, should be scheduled in the settings and at the times in which the target behavior typically occurs (e.g., classroom, home, community settings). For example, if a child frequently hits his classmates at recess, then the direct assessment should be conducted in the school during recess. This will maximize the likelihood that the observer will capture relevant and representative examples of the target behavior as they occur.

Functional analyses can be conducted in a few different locations. Often, functional analyses are conducted in structured and controlled settings, such as clinical settings, conference rooms, or observation rooms. This is so that all extraneous variables can be controlled so that the true relations between environmental events and behaviors can be discovered. However, this can result in situations that are difficult to compare to those that caregivers actually see in the natural setting and might result in interventions that are not relevant to the natural setting. In addition, these controlled settings aren't always available when a functional analysis is needed. Therefore, more recent research on functional analyses is often conducted in natural settings (e.g., classrooms, homes). The clinician conducting the assessment must balance experimental control and settings appropriately analogous to the naturally occurring environment when selecting the setting for the functional analysis.

Who Can Conduct an FBA?

Although no certification is required legally to complete an FBA, some training on the methods and process is necessary before one is conducted. Some professionals, such as Board Certified Behavior Analysts, receive training on conducting FBAs required as part of their certification process. Other professionals (e.g., clinical and school psychologists) may or may not have training in FBA methods, depending on where they received their education and clinical experience. It is important to remember that any professional should practice only within their expertise, so it is not recommended or ethical to conduct an FBA unless you have had adequate training and experience and are knowledgeable on the most recent advances in the research on assessment methodology.

What Is Needed Before You Start an FBA?

Prior to conducting an FBA, a clinician should learn as much as they can about the child that might be relevant to the assessment. This can be done as part of a comprehensive referral process or ecological assessment in which the clinician gathers information about current and previous educational settings, diagnoses, cognitive level, medical concerns, family history, educational records, and other relevant factors.

Additionally, a clinician should observe the behavior and collect baseline data to see how often the target behavior is occurring. In order to determine if the target behavior is typical of children of the same age, it would be beneficial to compare these baseline data to data collected of same-age typically developing peers. This is called collecting a normative sample and will not only determine if the target behavior is indeed problematic, but also help the clinician and caregivers select a reasonable and achievable goal based on the child's age. For example, if a parent of a preschool child with ASD refers the child for an FBA on whining, it would be important to determine if the child whines more often than children of the same age in similar settings to determine if this is a problem worthy of treatment resources.

It is also important to rule out any medical conditions that could be contributing to the target behavior. Often, when a person does not feel well or is in physical pain, tolerance for aversive situations can often be lowered and thus reasonably evoke challenging behavior. Instead of conducting an FBA, this challenging behavior might be more permanently eliminated by fixing the medical or physical condition. Think about how you felt the last time you went to work sick. Were you more likely to be irritable, snap at coworkers, whine, and so on? Examples of common physical conditions that are often found to contribute to the display of problem behaviors in children with ASD could be gastrointestinal issues such as acid reflux or irritable bowel syndrome, sleep or feeding disorders, seasonal allergies, or being in need of corrective vision or hearing devices. If a medical or physical condition is a significant contributor to problem behavior, often times addressing this condition can create a more lasting change in the behavior. If the target behavior is addressed, but not an underlying physical condition, then another problem behavior might arise in its place until the physical condition is eliminated.

How Do You Conduct an FBA?

The steps of the functional behavioral assessment and intervention involve using the scientific method, also referred to as the problem solving model. Problem Identification, Problem Analysis, Intervention Development, and Intervention Evaluation are the steps involved in problem-solving and are the logic behind the functional behavioral assessment process. Different types of a functional behavioral assessment can be utilized at different stages of the problem-solving model. The following section will describe this problem-solving model and then in Chapter 4 the process of intervention development and progress monitoring will be described in greater detail.

Problem Identification

Identification of the problem is the essential first step of an FBA and involves prioritizing areas for concern in relation to the referral question. The goal of a functional behavioral assessment is to develop a function-based intervention, so it is essential to have an identification of the problem, the behavior's impact on the environment and adaptive functioning of the child, as well as prioritizing which behaviors to target. Often, a referral question will include many aspects of difficulty, so the key is to prioritize which behavior(s) are a significant interfering factor to target, as it may not be realistic to target every behavior of concern during an initial functional behavioral assessment.

The first step of problem identification is to operationally define the target behavior as well as prioritize specific behaviors on which to intervene. An *operational definition* involves specifically stating what a target behavior *looks* like as well as what environmental events surround the behavior. The environmental factors affecting the behavior might not be evident until the functional behavioral assessment is completed, so the initial operational definition may mainly consist of a description of the topography of the behavior (what the behavior looks like). For example, let's take a target behavior of disruption. Disruptive behavior will look different for specific children, and adults will have different perceptions of what defines disruptive behavior. It may or may not include any combination of throwing items, writing on furniture, tipping furniture, or ripping materials, and these behaviors may occur in a variety of contexts with a variety of consequences. This is precisely why defining the behavior in overt, observable, and measurable terms is an essential first step. A good rule for an operational definition is that another person should be able to observe the child and collect data on the target behavior with accuracy, and it should include clear language with examples and nonexamples. In other words, the operational definition should be clear, concise, and complete (Cooper, Heron, & Heward, 2007).

When developing the operational definition, the clinician should directly observe the behavior as well as ask specific questions of those who have witnessed the behavior. These questions may include: What does the behavior look like? How often does it occur? In what contexts does it occur? What is the severity of the behavior? These steps will help to develop an operational definition that can be measured during the functional behavioral assessment. An example of disruptive behavior defined in measurable and observable terms is as follows: Disruptive behavior is defined as kicking walls, screaming (above normal speaking level), banging fists on furniture, usually displayed after an academic task is presented.

While defining what a behavior looks like is an essential first step, often, parents and teachers may get caught up with the many topographies of target behaviors and not necessarily the function of that behavior. Behaviors that look very different may serve the same behavioral function and therefore could be included in the same operational definition. When deciding whether to include behaviors as part of one operational definition, rather than separate behaviors, one should confirm through a functional behavioral assessment, that the behaviors are part of the same functional response class (i.e., the different topographies of the behavior serve the same function). For example, a child may scream and hit his mother when he doesn't want to eat his vegetables; both screaming and hitting could serve the same function of escape from eating vegetables and thus could both be included in an operational definition.

After an operational definition is determined, *baseline* data should be collected on the target behavior. Collecting baseline data involves collecting the current rates of the target behavior in the different contexts which it occurs. Determining the current rates of occurrence is important to validate the problem (i.e., what are the current rates, severity, disruption to the environment) as well as to later evaluate the effectiveness of the intervention derived from the functional behavioral assessment. Data should be collected in the natural environment and in the different contexts where the behavior occurs. These data can be collected via direct third-party observation (e.g., by a behavior analyst or school psychologist) as well as direct observation by teachers, parents, and staff. Permanent products that have been collected such as suspensions, incident reports, and performance on academic tasks can also be included and reviewed but should not be the sole data used in an evaluation of the intervention's effectiveness.

Types of data collected may include frequency—how long a behavior occurs, duration—how often a behavior occurs, latency—the amount of time it takes the behavior to start following a prompt, as well as percent of interval data. Refer to the assessment and progress monitoring sections for more detail on data-collection tools and use.

Problem Analysis

Indirect Assessment

During the problem identification stage of the FBA, the goal is to identify target behavior(s) of concern and validate the problem through the collection of baseline data, as well as begin to develop initial hypotheses of function. Indirect assessment methods involve the completion of rating scales and interviews about the problem behavior, and the context in which it occurs, from those that observe the target behaviors most frequently.

When conducting the indirect assessment, clinicians should interview individuals who have observed the behavior across environments including parents, teachers, paraprofessionals, or other school personnel or family members. It is important to choose informants that are able to provide detailed information on the behavior of concern and the environmental variables present when the behavior occurs.

Behavioral interviews, such as the Capitalize Behavioral Assessment can provide detail on the behavior of concern, events that occur before the behavior (antecedents), as well as events that occur after the behavior (O'Neill et al., 2015). Additionally, behavior interviews seek to determine relevant setting events including biological and environmental variables that may be contributing to the target behavior. The main advantage of structured interviews such as the FAI is that the information provided can help guide when, where, and what to observe during direct observations. Structured interviews also provide information used to develop a hypothesis that can be further developed and tested through direct assessment and FA. Other similar interview forms can be found in the literature.

Behavioral rating scales such as the Motivation Assessment Scale (MAS) and the Capitalize Behavioral Assessment are useful for further developing hypotheses on the environmental variables that may be maintaining the behavior of concern (Durand & Crimmins, 1988; Iwata, DeLeon, & Roscoe, 2013). These closed-ended instruments are quick and easy to complete and provide useful information on potential functions of behavior, but as with all of the indirect tools listed, should only be used as one piece of the FBA. Recent research indicates that indirect assessment instruments (i.e., FAST) agree with more controlled and systematic analogue FA results in only 63.8 percent of cases (Iwata, DeLeon, & Roscoe, 2013).

The information gathered through indirect assessment via the use of record review, interviews, and rating scales can help to develop the necessary information to guide direct assessments, behavior observations, and FAs. These data should be summarized in a narrative description, which includes any average scores from rating scales.

Descriptive Assessment

Through indirect assessment, data have been collected to help narrow the focus and gain some information about the context in which the behavior occurs. Using this information, the next step in problem identification, namely descriptive assessment, can be initiated. Descriptive assessment involves direct observation of the target behavior within the context which it occurs. Determining which behaviors to observe and when should be guided by the data collected from the indirect assessment. The methods and tools for observation range from more broad open-ended tools where data are collected on a wide range of aspects of the environment, to more narrow closed-ended tools where data are collected only on specific behaviors and aspects of the environment. Which data-collection tool is used will depend on the goal of the observation, who will be collecting the data, and the questions the examiner would like answered.

Sometimes the tool that will provide the most information about the environment is an open-ended ABC (Antecedent-Behavior-Consequence) narrative tool. This involves the examiner recording everything observed about the antecedents and consequences of the behavior, and any other relevant information observed. An advantage of an open-ended tool is the breadth of the information provided, a disadvantage is that this type of interview is not easily completed unless this is the observer's only responsibility (e.g., a teacher cannot easily complete and teach a lesson at the same time). The following is an example of an entry on an ABC narrative data sheet.

Time and activity	Antecedent	Behavior	Consequence
9 am Morning Circle Time.	Direction to sit down.	Yelled "Shut up!"	Teacher asked student to leave circle time.

Structured ABC recording is similar to narrative recording; however, collection of antecedents and consequences occurs in a more structured format. On a structured ABC recording form, there are specific categories of antecedents, behaviors, and consequences that can be easily circled or checked instead of written. Some structured ABC forms are available for use in the literature such as the Structured ABC Checklist (O'Neill et al., 2015). Others can be developed by clinicians to be individualized to specific children. This allows for ease of data collection, in that a teacher or paraprofessional may be able to collect data on antecedents and consequences simply by circling or checking the antecedent and consequence observed while teaching. Following is an example of an individualized structured ABC form.

Time and activity	Antecedent	Behavior	Consequence
Time: 10 am Activity: ☐ Academic ☐ Lunch ☑ Specials	☐ Work demand delivered ☐ Preferred item or activity removed ☑ Low attention situation	☑ Aggression ☐ Property destruction ☐ Self-injury ☐ Screaming	☐ Work delayed or removed ☐ Preferred item delivered ☑ Attention delivered

Name: _____   Month: _____

Behavior: _____

Definition: _____

☐ Behavior did NOT occur   ☐ Behavior occurred 1-5 times
☒ Behavior occurred 5 or more times

Days of the month

Time	1	2	3	4	5	6	7	8	9	10	11	12	13	14	15	16	17	18	19	20	21	22	23	24	25	26	27	28	29	30	31
6:00 AM																															
6:30 AM																															
7:00 AM																															
7:30 AM																															
8:00 AM					/						/								/					/							
8:30 AM																															
9:00 AM			/														/														
9:30 AM																															
10:00 AM	/													/	/												/				
10:30 AM																															
11:00 AM																															
11:30 AM																															
12:00 PM																															
12:30 PM	/	X		/	X		/		X		/		/	X	/	/	X		/	X		/	X	/		X	/		X	/	
1:00 PM	/	X				/	/					X		/	X				/	/			X			X		/	/		
1:30 PM																															
2:00 PM													/												/						
2:30 PM																															
3:00 PM	/													/	/													/			

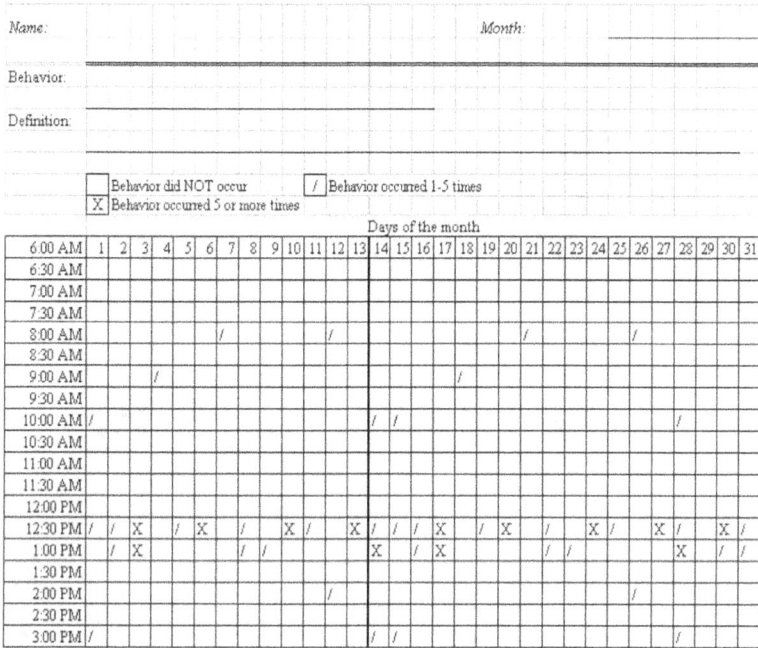

Figure 3.3 *This figure is a scatterplot of challenging behavior depicting a pattern of the target behavior occurring at a specific time of day*

Similarly, scatterplot data sheets can aid the clinician in identifying possible correlations between the target behavior and temporal patterns or events. For example, using the scatter plot shown in Figure 3.3, a clinician may be able to see a pattern in that the target behavior typically occurs during lunch time.

Narrative and structured ABC data should be summarized as the percentage of times the target behavior occurred following each antecedent observed, and percentage of times each consequence observed followed the target behavior. These results are typically graphed in a bar graph format. For example, Figure 3.4 shows the data collected on antecedents and consequences.

More sophisticated direct assessments could include sequential analyses or conditional probabilities in which the clinician calculates the probability that a target behavior is related to certain environmental events by determining how often events occur in a temporal pattern (e.g., Vollmer,

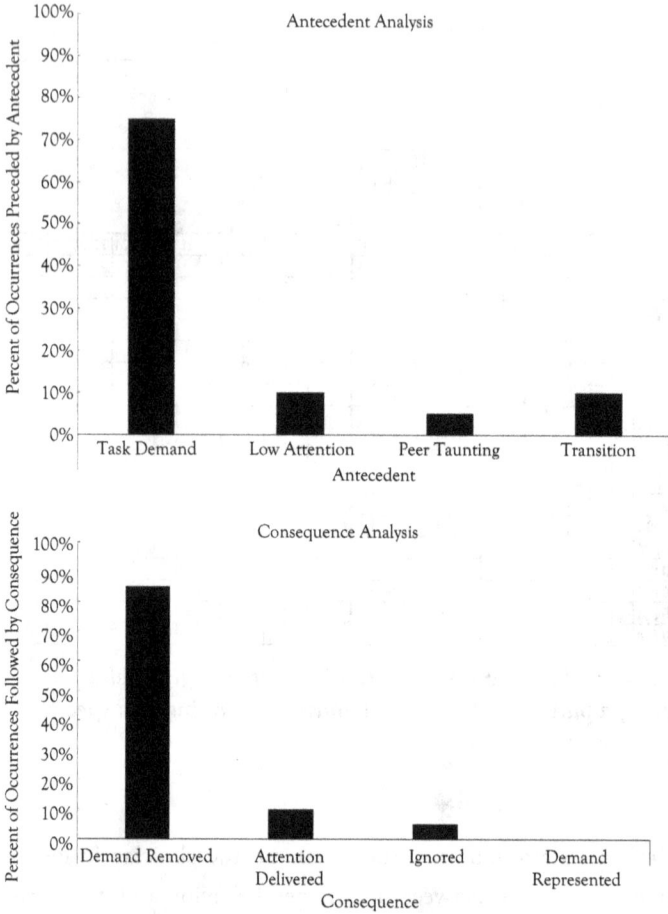

Figure 3.4 Graphs depicting the percentage of antecedents and consequences that occurred across all instances of challenging behavior observed

Borrero, Wright, Van Camp & Lalli, 2001; Martens, DiGennaro, Reed, Szczech, & Rosenthal, 2008). Specifically a clinician could calculate and compare the probability that the target behavior occurs given a specific antecedent to the probability that the target behavior occurs in the absence of that antecedent. Or the probability that a specific environmental event occurs following the target behavior (consequence) can be compared to the probability that the event occurs overall in the environment. For example, how often does aggression follow a time period where the child is left alone with no attention and then followed by attention, versus how often does aggression occur in other contexts and how often is attention delivered overall. These types of analyses can help the clinician to be more confident that certain events that occur in the environment are related to the target behavior, but often require additional training.

Functional Analysis

Data collected by indirect and direct assessment methods should help the clinician to develop a hypothesis of the target behavior. An essential last step in the problem-solving model is to test the hypothesis. Testing of the hypothesis can be done by contriving variables designed to evoke the behavior (FA) or observation of the behavior in response to the antecedents hypothesized (trigger analysis) (Cipani & Schock, 2011).

An FA is a type of functional behavioral assessment methodology that involves systematically manipulating environmental variables to determine the function of a target behavior. An FA can be used to test or confirm the clinician's hypothesis of the behavioral function. In an FA, the clinician exposes the child to different conditions and measures the rate of the target behavior to determine under which conditions it is most likely. This is not dissimilar to an allergy test where the child is exposed to different allergens to discover what stimuli result in allergic reactions. Iwata et al., (1982/1994) described an analogue FA that has been used as a model in an article first published in 1982 and then reprinted in 1994.

In an analogue FA, a clinician will expose the child to a demand condition, an attention condition, an alone condition, and a control condition and measure the rate of problem behavior that occurs in these different contexts (Iwata et al., 1982/1994). In the demand condition, the child is continuously presented with moderately difficult tasks and contingent upon the target behavior, the tasks are removed. This condition tests the hypothesis that the target behavior is maintained by escape from the task. In the attention condition, the child is ask to play quietly while the therapist works and the therapist does not provide any attention to the child unless the target behavior occurs. If and when the target behavior occurs, brief attention (usually in the form of a reprimand) is delivered immediately. Then attention is again removed until the next instance of the target behavior. This condition tests the hypothesis that the target behavior is maintained by attention from the adult therapist. In the alone condition, there are no demands, toys, or attention provided to the child and this condition is designed to test an automatic reinforcement function. In the control condition, the child is given his or her favorite toys and frequent attention from the adult therapist. This is a comparison condition to which the data in the other conditions are compared. These conditions are typically conducted in a controlled setting and are repeated until a pattern emerges on a graphical display of the data. The data are then displayed in a graph depicting the total frequency of the target behavior in each session organized by the condition to determine in which condition the problem behavior occurred most frequently. For example, the hypothetical data in Figure 3.5 show that the highest rates of the target behavior occur in the attention condition, confirming that the target behavior is maintained by access to adult attention.

A major advantage of an FA is it can provide a clear demonstration of behavioral function which can aid in the confident selection of the most effective function-based intervention. A qualified professional should design and conduct the FA to ensure the assessment is designed

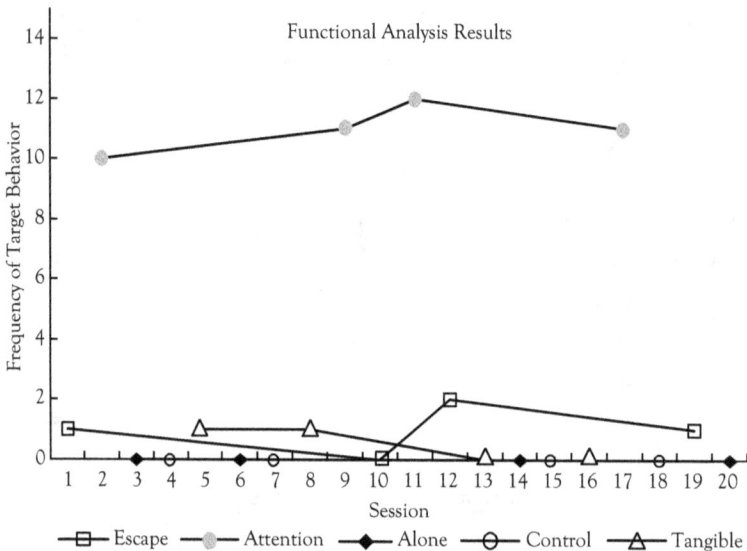

Figure 3.5 This figure depicts a functional analysis graph showing an access to attention function

appropriately and conducted with ethical integrity. Some disadvantages include the need for training and expertise, the time and resources for conducting, and the risks involved in increasing the rate of the target behavior. If the challenging behavior is a dangerous one, such as aggression or self-injury, there is a risk of injury in conducting the FA, as the target behavior is likely to increase under at least one of the conditions. This risk can be minimized by using safeguards such as termination criteria, protective equipment, and condition modifications. However, only a qualified professional trained in conducting FAs should design and implement this type of assessment following the analysis of the risks involved in each specific assessment context.

There are several modified versions of the analogue FA that can be utilized when appropriate. A tangible condition can be added in which a preferred item is delivered contingent on the target behavior to test the hypothesis that access to the item is maintaining the target behavior. The FA can be conducted in the natural setting and could be initiated upon an instance of the target behavior to make it more likely to capture the natural events (e.g., a trial-based FA; Tarbox et al., 2004). Instead of collecting data on the rate of the target behavior, latency data can be collected and the session could be terminated after the first instance of the behavior (e.g., a latency-based FA; Thomason-Sassi, Iwata, Neidert, & Roscoe, 2011). This modification assumes that the condition with the shortest latency would indicate the behavioral function and could be used for more dangerous behavior. If the target behavior is too severe to let occur even once during a session, an FA can be conducted on a precursor behavior instead (Smith & Churchill, 2002). Clinicians should research these modifications by examining the research literature prior to conducting.

A trigger analysis can be conducted instead of an FA to test the hypothesis of function (Cipani & Schock, 2011). A trigger analysis is similar in the design and procedures to the FA described earlier except that only antecedents are manipulated, and not consequences. The consequence typically delivered in the natural setting is delivered in the analysis, but different antecedent conditions (e.g., task demands, lack of attention) are conducted to determine what typically "triggers" the target behavior. Figure 3.6 shows the FBA decision tree.

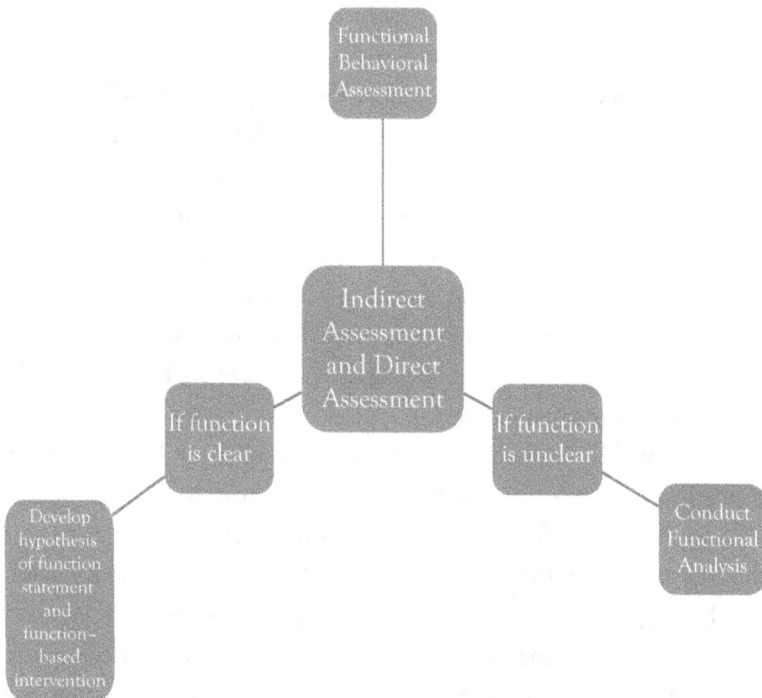

Figure 3.6 This figure depicts an FBA decision tree showing the different types of assessment that can be used

Data Analysis and Summary

Once all the types of data have been collected, it is important to analyze those data to develop a hypothesis of behavioral function. The hypothesis is typically presented in a sentence or a diagram describing the antecedents and setting events that occasion the target behavior and the reinforcer that maintains the target behavior. Often the results of each type of assessment (indirect, direct, and FA) are described in both narrative and graphic form in a functional behavioral assessment report. The report typically ends with the hypothesis of function statement or diagram and recommendations for intervention. Once all the data are analyzed, the clinician can write the statement based on the most commonly observed antecedents and consequences reported in the indirect assessments and observed in the direct assessments. Figure 3.7 is an example of a hypothesis of function statement and diagram for a behavior maintained by escape from demands.

Hypothesis statement: Sally engages in aggression in order to escape her independent Math assignments

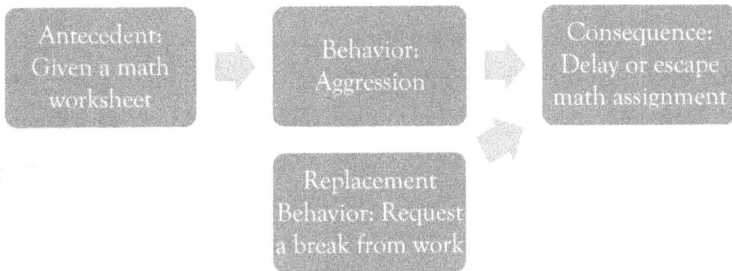

Figure 3.7 This figure depicts a hypothesis statement of behavioral function and hypothesis statement diagram

Complexities

Although the previous descriptions of the methods and results of a functional behavioral assessment may seem simple, human behavior can be complex. There can be many factors that may make it difficult to determine the function of a target behavior. There may be some relevant setting events or antecedents that are distant (e.g., past trauma, sleep deprivation, previous relationships) that might be difficult to detect. There may also be multiple functions of a target behavior. For example, a child may hit his peers in some situations to escape work in the classroom and in other situations to get adult attention. There may be medical (e.g., allergies, gastrointestinal issues), nutritional (e.g., food deprivation), and physical (e.g., fine motor deficits) issues that affect the target behavior as well. Also, functions may change over time. A well-trained and experienced clinician will take these complexities into account whenever applicable.

How Are Skills Assessed?

Initial and ongoing assessment of academic and functional skills is crucial before and during instruction, as it allows the clinician to choose appropriate academic interventions, determine the effectiveness of intervention strategies used, as well as identify modifications to interventions that may be needed. This is especially true given that ASD has no known cause or cure and therefore the best course of treatment is to address the child's individual skill deficits and behavioral excesses. However, students with ASD often present unique challenges when it comes to accurately assessing skill level. For example, children with ASD may have difficulty developing rapport with the examiner, have deficits in communication skills making it difficult for them to understand and communicate with the examiner, and may display challenging and/or repetitive behaviors that interfere with testing. Due to these challenges, typical standardized assessments do not always portray an accurate picture of present skill levels in children with ASD. It is important to understand the different types of skills that may need to be assessed as well as the different types of assessments available to develop the most accurate representation of the child.

In order to develop effective individualized teaching strategies, an instructor must first determine the child's current skill level. An instructor may need to assess many different types of skills in each learner. For example, an instructor may assess discrete skills (e.g., rapid skills that are easy to repeat such as color identification) or more complex skills (e.g., skills that include many related responses that occur in a sequence such as behavior sequences or chains). These discrete or complex skills may be related to academics (e.g., Math, reading, science), communication (e.g., making requests, holding conversations, commenting on events), social skills (e.g., playing with peers, problem solving), daily living skills (e.g., dressing, grooming, toileting, cooking, cleaning), prevocational skills (e.g., sorting, filing, cleaning), or recreation (e.g., play skills, leisure skills).

What Are the Types of Skills Assessments?

The two main types of skills assessment are summative and formative. Summative assessment refers to assessing the child's skill level at one point of time, such as at the end of instruction, to determine what they have learned by comparing it to a standard or criterion. Examples of summative assessment include norm-referenced and criterion-based assessments such as state-mandated tests, end of term exams, standardized tests, course grades, and so on. Formative assessment refers to monitoring a student's skills through ongoing (i.e., frequent and repeated) assessment so that the instructor can use the information to shape instructional decisions. Examples of formative assessments can include skill probes, situational tests, and curriculum-based measures (CBM).

There are some assessments that are commonly used with children diagnosed with ASD. One criterion-referenced assessment commonly used to assess language and social skills is the Verbal Behavior Milestones Assessment and Placement Program (VB-MAPP; Sundberg, 2008). This assessment assesses language and learning milestones typically observed in young children (ages birth to 4 years). The VB-MAPP has five components, a milestones assessment to provide an instructor with the learner's current skill level, a barriers assessment to identify common learning barriers, a transition assessment to aid in assessing readiness for less restrictive educational environments, a task analysis and skills tracking component, and an individualized education plan (IEP) placement and guide. The Assessment of Language and Learning Skills—Revised (ABLLS-R®; Partington, 2006) is a similar assessment, curriculum guide, and progress monitoring tool that assesses a variety of language, social, academic, self-help, and motor skills. Both assessments are based on B.F. Skinner's (1957) analysis of verbal behavior and can be used to determine skills to target for instruction as well as for ongoing progressing monitoring.

Another useful assessment for program development and progress monitoring is the Assessment of Functional Living Skills (AFLS®; Partington & Mueller, 2012). This tool assesses basic living skills, home skills, community participation, daily living, vocational, and school readiness skills. These are skills that can often be difficult to define and target for instruction but are crucial for success in many school, residential, community, recreational, and vocational settings. It is one of the only direct assessments of its kind for these types of skills, as many assessments of similar functional living skills are based on parent or staff report and thus subject to disadvantages such as issues with accuracy, biases, interpretations, and so on. Rating scale and interview assessments can be helpful as a starting place for program development, but should not be used for ongoing progress monitoring, as they are usually not accurate or sensitive enough to depict changes in skill levels. For example, the Vineland Adaptive Behavior Scales, Second Edition (Vineland™-II; Sparrow, Cichetti, & Balla, 2005) is a rating form given to parents or caregivers to assess current levels of communication, daily living skills, social skills, motor skills, and maladaptive behaviors. This assessment is a good starting place for instruction, but again, may not be sensitive enough to show changes in skill level due to instruction over time.

There are many assessments of social skills relevant for children with ASD available. Many common social skills assessments are based on parent and staff reports of how children with ASD interact with peers, as social skills tend to be difficult to directly observe. Several rating scales are available such as: Social Skills Improvement Scale (Gresham & Elliot, 2008), Social Responsiveness Scale (Constantino, 2005), Gilliam Autism Rating Scale—3rd Edition (Gilliam, 2014), Autism Social Skills Profile (Bellini, 2006), and Social Skills Improvement System (SSRS, Gresham & Elliot, 2008). In addition, many publically available social skills curricula have assessments built for initial assessment and progress monitoring, such as The Incredible Years (Webster-Stratton, 2005), Skill Streaming (McGinnis & Simpson, 2016), and Second Step (Committee for Children, 2017).

The assessment of academic skills of children with ASD may be conducted using curriculum-based measures (CBM) rather than standardized, summative assessment of abilities. While standardized measures have their value in providing information on broad and narrow abilities, CBM are beneficial in skills assessment as they provide information that can be easily translated to program development and progress monitoring. CBM can be repeated quickly and frequently for progress monitoring and relate directly to the learning materials. Additionally, CBM usually involve a small array of probe-type questions asked in a rapid manner to assess fluency in academic areas such as reading, Math, spelling, and so on. Results are graphed on an individual student's chart to indicate progress in a particular topic area. The probes may come directly from the texts or curriculum materials used from research on age-appropriate academic skills. The results of CBM provide an indicator of performance on a variety of skills that can be used to guide goal development and future programming. The results of the assessment can be related back to the curriculum to further establish goals and inform instruction. An example of a CBM is the DIBELS or Dynamic Indicators of Basic Early Literacy Skills (Dynamic Measurement Group, 2008). The DIBELS involves taking many short probes regarding reading and early literacy skills over repeated measurements to assess instruction effectiveness.

How Are Skills Assessments Conducted?

Regardless of the type of assessment used to determine skill level, there are some common assessment practices that can be used to help ensure accurate and valid measures of the learner's skill level. For example, during assessment, the test administrator should first develop rapport with the learner to gain trust and develop a history of compliance with instructions given by the administrator. The test administrator should ensure that all materials are ready when the testing time begins, and limit the testing time (which may need to be individualized) to avoid fatigue or challenging behavior resulting from waiting or slow pace of interactions. Testing should end on a successful note, in other words a correct response, to avoid frustration and task avoidance of future tests. The testing should be conducted in the natural environment, when possible, to determine application of functional skills in real-world settings. Additionally, generalization should also be assessed during the testing with the use of multiple examples, different types of materials, multiple settings, and multiple test administrators. For example, when testing self-help skills such as handwashing, the tests should be conducted in a variety of real-world sinks such as kitchens and bathrooms in which the child regularly washes his or her hands, within a variety of settings, and with a variety of testers.

In addition, skills should be assessed multiple times to ensure accurate representation of performance is obtained. For example, if skills were only assessed once and skill level was low, the assessor may not be confident that this was an accurate picture of performance, rather than low performance due to an illness, lack of rapport with the examiner, or other temporary condition that affected the performance. It may also be helpful to some children with ASD to start with skills that are easily completed by the student (e.g., skills the child has previously mastered) first, and then move to more difficult skills during the assessment. This could take advantage of "behavioral momentum" a principle in which behavior that is more difficult or less likely to occur is more probable if it follows easy or high probability behavior. This can help to establish a pattern of compliance with demands, and if a fast pace is used, could result in more skills tested in a shorter period of time. Finally, during assessments, correct or accurate responding should not result in reinforcement. This is so that assessors can obtain an accurate picture of skill level under nonteaching conditions. In other words, if correct responses are reinforced, this is teaching and not assessment and could result in performance that is affected by the assessor's behavior instead of an accurate picture of purely independent performance.

Functional Behavioral Assessment of Academic Behavior

A student may be able to complete a specific skill, but for some reason, does not perform the skill in all the necessary environments. For example, perhaps a student has learned to properly wash their hands, but doesn't wash their hands after using the restroom or before meals or when confronted with a new type of sink. In another example, perhaps a student has learned to write their name but doesn't do so legibly when asked to write their name on a worksheet. A different situation might involve a teacher that has been instructing a student on the same skill for quite a long time, without demonstration that the student is learning the skill. In other words, the student is having trouble learning how to do the skill. These examples show two different problems: a performance deficit and a skill deficit. Both of these types of situations are in need of intervention, but it is difficult to tell exactly what type of intervention would be most appropriate unless you know why the student is not learning or performing as expected.

A functional behavioral assessment, similar to that described in an earlier section to assess problem behavior, can be conducted to determine an appropriate academic intervention for poor academic performance (Daly et al., 1997). A functional behavioral assessment of academic performance involves the same conceptual analysis involved in a functional behavioral assessment of problem behavior. Specifically, the environmental variables affecting academic performance, such as events that happen before and after the academic task, are analyzed to determine specific problems to address in academic intervention.

To conduct a functional behavioral assessment on academic behavior, the assessor would gather indirect and direct information on environmental variables by interviewing students, teachers, and peers, and then observing the student perform the tasks while collecting data on antecedents and consequences. In addition, relevant antecedents and consequences could be manipulated to determine the conditions in which the student will display the skill versus conditions in which they will not. Specifically, brief sessions in which interventions addressing several hypothesized issues (e.g., motivational issues, instructional level matching, fluency building) are probed in a multielement or brief multielement design to determine which will be most effective (see Daly et al., 1997 for details).

For example, a functional behavioral assessment may identify that a student can do a skill but lacks the motivation to perform the skill in all the appropriate contexts. Perhaps a student has difficulty reading fluently in certain situations. An assessment might reveal that the student is able to read fluently, so a motivational intervention such as providing choice of reading materials or incentives to read might be appropriate. If the student is unable to read the given current instructional methods, then an assessment might reveal that the reading problem is due to lack of practice in fluency, or poor generalization of phonemic skills, or poor match between difficulty level and skill level. These assessment findings would result in very different interventions.

All of the preceding assessment methods should produce results that are used to guide teachers and instructors to choose appropriate learning goals, appropriate instructional strategies, and appropriate instructional interventions.

Strategies for Progress Monitoring and Tracking Meaningful Benefit

As described earlier, formative evaluation is often more useful than summative evaluation for measuring progress. Although, some of the summative measures described in the skills assessment section could be used repeatedly (e.g., once per academic quarter or once per academic year), they are often too time consuming to do often enough to make data-based changes to interventions to ensure effective instruction. In addition, many of the summative measures may not measure specific target skills in a way that would be sensitive enough to capture small changes in learning. Formative evaluative measures can and should be tailored to the specific target behavior being measured. A teacher or clinician should carefully select data collection strategies that will be most accurate and

sensitive for monitoring progress in the target behavior, whether that target behavior is a skill to increase or a problem behavior to decrease. Data
collection will also determine if the goal of the intervention is met and
if the skill or behavior change has been generalized to all the appropriate
settings, stimuli, and response topographies.

What Is Appropriate Data Collection?

Appropriate and sensitive data collection refers to a method of directly
observing and quantifying behavioral performance repeatedly over time
in order to assess changes in the target behavior. Data collection is the
most effective way to measure progress before, during, and after any
behavioral intervention. In order to collect data that can be used to effectively measure progress during an intervention, the relevant dimension of
the behavior must be selected (e.g., frequency, duration, rate), defined,
and measured using the most appropriate data-collection method (e.g.,
event recording, timing). The chosen data-collection method should meet
three criteria: accuracy (as compared to a true value), reliability (consistent measures obtained when repeated), and validity (measures the
dimension of interest directly). For example, to measure reading fluency,
the relevant dimension of interest would be rate of words read aloud, and
an appropriate data-collection method would be to take event recording
(count) of the words read correctly and divide by the number of minutes
it took to read them (i.e., calculate rate of words read per minute). This
data-collection method should be assessed for accuracy, reliability, and
validity (Cooper, Heron, & Heward, 2007). Another example, to assess
accuracy, the reading task could be video-recorded and the words could be
observed again to match the words to proper pronunciation models. To
assess reliability, the same video showing the same instances of the behavior could be observed by the same observer multiple times to ensure the
same rate of reading is detected across repeated measurement. To assess
validity, it would be necessary to ensure that the rate of words read per
minute is a valid construct for measuring reading. Similarly, measuring
the frequency of classroom disruption could be assessed for accuracy, reliability, and validity in the same ways. In addition to accuracy, reliability,
and validity, the data-collection method should be sensitive enough to

detect even small changes in progress. Also, generalization and maintenance probe data should be collected to ensure the behavior has changed in all appropriate settings, with all appropriate stimuli and to all appropriate responses.

Additionally, interobserver agreement should also be collected and calculated on the data used in decision making to enhance believability of the data. Interobserver agreement data involve a secondary observer taking the same data as a primary data collector and then comparing the two data sets for consistency. This can help the clinician find some common issues associated with ongoing frequent data collection (e.g., therapist drift, poor operational definitions, data-collection methods that are too cumbersome). Various methods of interobserver agreement calculations exist and should be individualized to your data-collection method (see Cooper, Heron, & Heward, 2007 for a thorough description).

Why Should Data Be Collected?

Data should be collected regularly on any behavior targeted for intervention to ensure the intervention is effective and progress is made and maintained. Frequent data collection can be used to make decisions about continuing, modifying, discontinuing or changing interventions. Data can also determine when a clinical, or instructional goal is met and the intervention can be faded. Data collection can also validate the rationale for resource allocation in terms of staff time and salary, and materials used for intervention. Ensuring interventions are effective and making data-based decisions regarding intervention selection and use can hold teachers and clinicians accountable to the client, the client's family, teachers, peers, and any other stakeholders. Data in the form of generalization probes in all the appropriate settings and situations can determine what additional exemplars should be used in instruction to ensure the skill can be practiced in all necessary situations.

Who Should Collect Data for Progress Monitoring?

Data collectors should include anyone that has the ability to frequently observe the target behaviors. This may be the clinician (e.g., behavior analyst, school psychologist) but most likely will be teachers, teachers' assistants, aides, and one-to-one staff that are constantly with the child. Typically, these are individuals that are implementing the intervention as well. This can have advantages and disadvantages that should be considered. For example, while individuals directly working with the child are most conveniently available during the key observation times, it may be difficult to implement some complex interventions while simultaneously collecting data. Anyone collecting data should be trained to competency on the data collection procedures. This training should include a review of the operational definition and data-collection tool (e.g., data sheet) as well as practice data collection sessions in which they collect data with at least 80 to 90 percent interobserver agreement.

How Should Progress Be Monitored?

The first step of formative assessment data collection involves developing an operational definition of the target behavior. The operational definition should be clear and easy to understand, concise, objective, and include examples and nonexamples that the data collector may encounter. The development of the operational definition is an important process as this definition will determine which topographies of the target behavior will be included and excluded in the data collection process. For example, if the target behavior, aggression, is defined as, "instances or attempts of hitting another person with a closed fist from at least 6 inches away, not including slapping or fist bumps," this includes hitting, and excludes fist bumps. However, this also excludes other topographies of aggression that might serve the same behavioral function such as, pinching, kicking, biting, and so on. Hence, an operational definition may need to be refined several times to ensure it captures all instances of the relevant behavior.

Once an operational definition is developed, the clinician must select the appropriate measurement dimension. For example, if the target behavior is aggression, as defined earlier, frequency (count) would likely be the relevant dimension. However, if the target behavior were screaming, perhaps frequency and duration (length of time) may be relevant. For academic responding, a clinician may be interested in the rate (count per unit of time) or accuracy (percentage correct) of a behavioral response.

CBM often measure accuracy and fluency of academic behavior. Other dimensions that may be relevant to certain contexts include inter-response time (time between responses), latency (time from a stimulus to the response), and percentage (e.g., percent of opportunities, percent independent responses, percent correct). Once the appropriate dimension is identified, a data-collection method can be selected that fits that dimension as well as data-collection tools (e.g., data sheets or electronic systems). For example, if frequency or rate is the dimension of interest, an event recording or tally system may be appropriate. The data-collection method selected should take into account the nature of the behavior (e.g., does it happen too often and quickly to count accurately?), the responsibilities of the data collector (e.g., is the teacher teaching a lesson while she is expected to collect data?), and the complexity of the data-collection method (e.g., is it too complex or time consuming?). Many practical strategies have been used to make data collection easier such as moving beads on a bracelet, using a pitch counter, moving pennies from one pocket to the other, and so on.

Some data-collection strategies, such as interval recording, may be more practical but less accurate than frequency or duration recording as they give estimates of these dimensions of behavior. There are three types of interval data: partial interval, whole interval, and momentary time sampling. In each of these types of recording, the observation period is divided into time intervals (e.g., a 1-hour observation could be divided into 60 1-minute intervals) and a timing device is used to signal to the observer when the interval is over. In partial interval recording, the observer marks the interval if the behavior has occurred at all during that interval (regardless of frequency). In whole interval, the behavior must be occurring throughout the entire duration of the interval in order for the interval to be marked. In momentary time sampling, the interval is marked if the behavior is occurring at the second the interval ends. Interval data are summarized as percentage of intervals and give an estimate of how much of the behavior occurred during the observation.

Once the data-collection method is determined, generalization and maintenance probes should also be planned. For example, if a child is taught Math skills in the classroom using flash cards, can he or she use those same skills in the cafeteria when paying for lunch, in the store when shopping for items, and using numbers of different sizes? Can they write and say the answers as well as point to the answer? Prior to beginning data collection, the instructor should determine all the appropriate settings and stimuli that the child will encounter in regards to the skill and collect data if the skills are demonstrated in those ways prior to and after data collection.

When Should Data Be Collected?

Baseline data, or data on the target behavior prior to any intervention, should be collected before any changes are made to behavioral or academic programming. These data will be compared to post-intervention data to assess effectiveness. Data should be collected frequently throughout the implementation of the intervention to determine if any modifications to the intervention are necessary. Frequent and repeated measures are the hallmark of applied behavior analysis, as they indicate exactly when changes in behavior occur. Data should also be collected after an intervention is removed or withdrawn (i.e., after a behavioral goal is achieved) to determine that the target behavior is maintained at the appropriate level. For example, if the target behavior is aggression displayed by a child with ASD in a special education classroom, data could be collected for at least 3 days prior to the intervention being implemented, daily during the intervention, and then probed at 1 month, 3 months, and 6 months post-intervention (once the aggression is low enough to remove the intervention). Similarly, if the target behavior is words read aloud correctly, data could be collected for at least 3 days prior to the intervention being implemented, daily during the intervention, and then probed at 1 month, 3 months, and 6 months post-intervention removal.

To assess the effectiveness of any intervention, data should be collected and interventions should be implemented in a systematic fashion. In other words, environmental conditions should be held constant with no changes other than the intervention, to assess if any changes in behavior are due to the intervention and not some other variable. Data should be reviewed for stability prior to implementing any changes in the intervention, again to ensure the intervention is responsible for changes in the target behavior and not some other extraneous variable (e.g., sleep, eating, staffing changes). Ideally, data would be collected during the arrangement of a single case experimental design (Tawney & Gast, 1984). For example, the intervention may be one that could be implemented following baseline, and then removed and implemented again to ensure that the intervention was responsible for the change in behavior. This is called a withdrawal (or sometimes referred to as a reversal) design. Another single case design that is used frequently in school and home settings is the multiple baseline design. In this design, baseline data are collected on the target behavior in three settings with three children or in three similar behaviors. Then the implementation of the intervention is staggered in time across these different contexts. This design aims to show the intervention, and not some other variable that might have been changed at the same time, is responsible for the change in the target behavior. Other experimental designs are also available to meet the needs of many applied situations. The clinician should seek to develop skills in these and other experimental designs, including the clinical and experimental advantages and disadvantages of each and when each should be used prior to implementing.

Finally, maintenance data should be collected after interventions are discontinued to determine that no skill regression occurs and that behavior is maintained at the appropriate levels. Maintenance data can be collected days, weeks, months, and years following intervention. This can indicate if further intervention is necessary due to regression.

What Should Be Done with the Data?

As data are collected, they should be graphed in a visual display (typically a line graph) that can be viewed quickly and conveniently by the clinician or staff working with the child on a daily or at least weekly basis. Visual analysis of the graph should include assessing the data for its level, trends, variability, stability, and immediacy of effect. Looking at all of these aspects of the data could aid in determining whether the intervention is effective. Viewing the intervention data and comparing it to baseline data could determine if changes need to be made or if the intervention should continue as is. Changes may include modifying the intervention, changing the intervention, or fading or discontinuing intervention due to meeting the target goal.

CHAPTER 4

Treatment

Just as assessment is focused on individual deficits and excesses, interventions should be individualized in design to meet each specific target area. This usually requires multiple types of interventions in a package. The foundational principles of applied behavior analysis should be rooted throughout any type of intervention. An example of this would be that reinforcement of appropriate behavior should be included in any intervention. Reinforcement, as described in Chapter 3, is a consequence delivered after a behavior that increases the future probability of that behavior. In order to ensure a behavior continues, it must be reinforced, specifically, reinforcement must be arranged for any desired behaviors. This reinforcement may naturally occur in the environment or be specially engineered. Reinforcers, by definition, are effective. If a consequence is delivered after a response and it does not result in the future display of that behavior, then it is not a reinforcer, even if it was intended to function as one. For example, if stickers are delivered after correct responding in class, but correct responding does not increase, then it is not a reinforcer. Therefore, special care must be taken to ensure that effective reinforcers are used. Individual preferences shift constantly, so it is critical that preferences are assessed just prior to intervention to determine what stimuli might function as reinforcers. For example, some children like praise, some like edible items, and some like activities. Preferences can be assessed via informal questionnaires or formal preference assessments in which stimuli are presented, in various formats, to determine a child's preference (e.g., DeLeon & Iwata, 1996; Fisher et al., 1996).

For children with Autism Spectrum Disorder (ASD), many social interactions such as hugs, high fives, and praise are not effective reinforcers. Therefore, although using food or toys as reinforcers may not be preferable within interventions due to issues such as health, age appropriateness, and satiation, it may be necessary to use these types of reinforcers until more appropriate long-term reinforcers are established.

In addition, the desired effects of any intervention should have long-term benefits as well as benefits that spread to other areas not directly targeted. This is called maintenance and generalization. Any intervention should include strategies that promote generalization and maintenance of effects across settings, situations, responses, and time. Some common strategies to promote generalization include highlighting common elements between the instructional and generalization settings, teaching self-management strategies, varying irrelevant contextual stimuli during teaching, teaching sufficient exemplars of topics or items, using sequential modifications in teaching, using intermittent and delayed reinforcement similar to the natural environment, and reinforcing novel responses (Stokes & Baer, 1977).

Finally, all interventions should utilize strengths to remediate weaknesses. While interventions are often developed and implemented because there are deficits present in some area, just like everyone, children with ASD possess numerous talents and strengths. Recognizing and incorporating these strengths is an essential component in any intervention. Following are some examples of how to utilize strengths when designing interventions:

Common difficulty	Associated strength	Strategy
Social interaction and understanding of social cues	Excellent visual memory	Using pictures, cartoons, social stories, to teach social interaction and social cues
Difficulty initiating or sustaining conversation	Strong special interests	Use special interest topic to facilitate social engagement or parallel play
Difficulty with language comprehension	Strong memory skills	Language should be short and concrete, paired with gestures, pictures, and modeling
Intense preoccupation with special interest	Motivation, patience, and determination	Use special interest to engage child in conversation with others
Rule governed	Rule governed	Teach safety rules and teach flexibility

Communication

Why Should Communication Be a Main Focus of Intervention for Children with ASD?

Communication is one of the core deficits of ASD and therefore should always be a primary target for instruction (APA, 2013). Communication is a pivotal skill (Koegel & Frea, 1993) that underlies many other skill areas, and by teaching communication, a child is exposed to a wide variety of reinforcers. Once effective communication is learned, a child can begin to ask for things they need or want. Communication is also an essential component to effective socialization, one of the other core deficits of ASD. Finally, a lack of communication is often the underlying reason behind the demonstration of challenging behavior.

Who Should Participate in Communication Instruction?

Once communication goals and modalities are established, everyone in the child's environment should participate in communication instruction. Individuals in the child's network should model communication as well as prompt communication during naturally occurring opportunities. Parents, teachers, caregivers, siblings, and peers can all participate in language instruction by contriving and capturing opportunities for the child to use language skills. For example, during lunch, a caregiver can prompt requests for particular foods, needed utensils, drinks, and so on. During play, peers and siblings can prompt requests to interrupt play and then prompt for requests to continue or requests for needed or wanted items, as well as prompt appropriate conversation. Teachers and parents can move preferred items into difficult to reach locations, requiring the child to ask for assistance. In addition, these friends and family can model the appropriate modality that the child uses (e.g., vocal speech, sign language) by labeling items and providing model prompts for requests and conversations.

What Types of Communication Skills Should Be Taught?

Communication is a broad term that can describe many different types of modalities and messages. There are a variety of reasons why children may need to communicate: to ask for things, to label things, to respond to questions, to repeat things others say, to read aloud, and so on. These different functions of communication should be analyzed separately, since just because a child can label an item, doesn't mean they can then ask for it when they need it (Lamarre & Holland, 1985). Skinner (1957) developed a method of categorizing and analyzing language in its different functions that can be very helpful in teaching language, especially to children with ASD. The use of Skinner's analysis of verbal behavior has been useful in the language instruction of children with ASD due to its unique view of seeing each word or phrase for the function it serves as opposed to just the meaning. The specific implications of this in the assessment and intervention of children with ASD include the ability to analyze complex language deficits and splintered skills to teach a fully functional repertoire (Sundberg & Michael, 2001). Specifically, an instructor is able to break down language and teach functional communication by teaching units of language in the contexts in which they will be used. For example, instead of teaching a child to receptively and expressively communicate the word "water," an instructor could teach the word "water" in the context of asking for water, labeling water, and repeating the word water, to ensure the word water will be used in contexts in which it is needed.

In Skinner's (1957) analysis of verbal behavior, the functions of language are broken down into elementary verbal operants. He termed these "operants" due to the way they operate or function on the environment to highlight the differences in how they are used in functional language. Each operant has a different combination of antecedent, response topography, and reinforcer. The controlling antecedent for a mand is some sort of motivation (e.g., to satisfy a physical condition such as deprivation or access stimulation), the response is a request for an item and the reinforcing consequence is access to that specific item. For example, a child may mand for scissors when an art project calls for cutting, and the result of the mand is the delivery of scissors by another person. When a child sees an item or event and as a result describes it and this response is then reinforced with social reinforcement from another person such as confirmation, this is a tact. For example, if a child sees an airplane, says, "Airplane!" and a listener responds with, "Wow that is a big airplane!"—this is a tact. An intraverbal is displayed when a child responds verbally with a verbal stimulus that is dissimilar from the response. Intraverbals are essential in answering questions and holding conversations. For example, if a teacher says, "What do you want for lunch?" and a child responds with, "Pizza!"—this is an intraverbal. Alternatively, an echoic response occurs in response to a verbal stimulus that is identical to the response. For example, when a teacher says, "Abracadabra!" and the child repeats it, this is an echoic. Some of the other verbal operants (i.e., listener responding, textual, copying text, and transcription) are described in the table below comparing the most common verbal operants described by Skinner (1957). Following is a breakdown of verbal operants (verbal units) described by Skinner:

Verbal operant	Antecedent controlling variable	Consequence	Example
Mand	Motivation	Access to the specific item	Child hasn't had a drink lately, says, "Water," and receives a drink of water
Tact	Nonverbal stimulus	Social reinforcement	Child sees an ocean, and says, "Water!" and peer says, "Yes!"
Echoic	Verbal stimulus identical to response	Social reinforcement	Teacher says, "Water," and child says, "Water" and teacher says, "Great, you said water!"
Intraverbal	Verbal stimulus different from response	Social reinforcement	Teacher says, "What is the ocean made of?" and child says, "Water" and teacher says, "Correct!"
Listener responding	Verbal instruction	Social reinforcement	Teacher says which one is water and child points to the cup of water and teacher says, "Great, that is a cup of water!"
Textual	Written verbal stimulus	Social reinforcement	Child sees the word "Water" written on the board and says, "Water" and teacher says, "That's right!"
Transcription	Spoken verbal stimulus	Social reinforcement	Teacher says, "Water," and child writes down, "Water" and gets an A+
Copying text	Written verbal stimulus similar to response	Social reinforcement	Child sees "Water" written and writes "Water" and teacher says, "Yes!"

The order of how these verbal operants are taught to children with ASD is also important. Many researchers agree that the mand should be the first verbal operant taught, as it is immediately useful to the speaker (Skinner, 1957; Sundberg & Partington, 1998; Sundberg & Michael, 2001). When a mand is performed, the consequence or reinforcer is access to whatever is specified by the mand. For example, a mand for water would result in access to water. Due to this immediately useful nature of the mand, it is often thought to be easier to acquire. Depending on the learner, echoics may need to be taught before mands so that the instructor can use the model of the word as a prompt to encourage the child to display the mand (e.g., a teacher can prompt a thirsty child to, "say water"). Mands, tacts, intraverbals, and other verbal operants are usually the focus of instruction simultaneously so that a fully functional language repertoire is established.

Vocal language is usually the first target of communication skills. However, in children with ASD that are nonverbal (estimates by the CDC approximate 50 percent), other methods of communication must be taught. There are two types of augmentative and alternative communication (AAC) methods typically used by children with ASD: selection-based and topography-based. Selection-based AACs involve a system where stimuli that represent different words or phrases are selected by the child by either touching, pointing, or selecting them. A common selection-based AAC is the Picture Exchange Communication System (PECS; Bondy & Frost, 2001; Frost & Bondy, 2002; Sulzer-Azaroff et al., 2009). PECS is a picture icon-based communication system, based on Skinner's analysis of verbal behavior, in which the child is first taught mands by selecting picture icons from a board or book and exchanging them with a listener. The early phases of PECS training use errorless teaching to teach mands and the later phases focus on tacting, intraverbals, and other verbal operants. A unique aspect of PECS is that it specifies a training model based on Skinner's analysis of verbal operants and lends itself nicely to designing a language program for children with ASD that allows for the complex variables that influence communication (Bondy, Tincani, & Frost, 2004). PECS has a large research base for its effectiveness in its use with children with ASD (Ganz et al., 2012) and has the advantage of the universal understandability for listeners. Other common selection-based AAC devices include voice output communication aids (VOCAs), in which a child presses buttons on a device that represent different words or phrases and then once a phrase or sentence is formed, the device can "speak" the words aloud for a listener. Many VOCAs have been proven effective in teaching children with ASD to communicate (Ramdoss et al., 2011). There are many companies that make devices or applications for electronic tablets such as iPads that act as VOCAs (e.g., Dynavox, PECS for iPad application, Proloquo2go).

Topography-based communication systems involve communication methods in which each word or phrase has a different topographical response. For example, in speech, each word has a different sound. In sign language, each word has a different sign. Sign language has been used extensively by children with ASD and has many advantages. Sign language has a built-in community, and is recognized as a true language with all the characteristics of complex language (e.g., systematic, symbolic, conventional, productive).

Some research has shown that topography-based systems are acquired more quickly by individuals with developmental disabilities for a variety of conceptual reasons (Sundberg & Sundberg, 1990). Potter and Brown (1997) completed a review of studies that taught selection-based and topography-based systems and found a pattern that topography-based communication systems may be easier to acquire. However, there is some argument that selection-based systems may be preferable due to the understandability by audiences and that the individual only needs to learn one physical response (i.e., pointing). It is more likely that the selection of the appropriate system is an individual decision that depends on a learner's current skill set, history of learning, and preferences.

Where Should Communication Instruction Occur?

Communication instruction should occur in all environments in which the child interacts with others. The skills of communication need to be demonstrated in every environment in which a child experiences; therefore, a child needs to learn to communicate in all possible environments. Every effort should be made to promote generalization and maintenance of communication skills taught. This would require communication learning opportunities, instructional trials, modeling, prompting, and reinforcement in all environments.

How Should Communication Skills Be Taught?

Communication should be taught using both contrived, formal instruction as well as using natural environment teaching (NET). There have been numerous studies addressing different methods of instruction for different types of language. From the literature on language and communication training with children with ASD, many common strategies and tips can be extracted. Some tips include:

1. Teach communication using Skinner's (1957) analysis of verbal behavior for a complete verbal repertoire. Sundberg & Partington (1998) provide a seminal manual for providing language instruction based on Skinner's (1957) analysis.

2. Teach mands first to provide immediate functional language for the learner (Sundberg & Partington, 1998).

3. When teaching mands, use a combination of contriving opportunities in the environment to evoke mands as well as capturing naturally occurring opportunities (Shafer, 1995). This should include incidental or NET, choice making, and the interrupted chain strategy in which tasks are interrupted so children can request they continue by requesting for needed items.

4. Teach the different functions of language (i.e., the verbal operants) separately. Just because you teach a word as a label, the child may not be able to use it as a request (Lamarre & Holland, 1985).

5. Use errorless teaching when possible to allow for efficient and effective learning (Sundberg & Partington, 1998).

6. Use language assessments that test for the different functions of communication (i.e., the different verbal operants) to create communication goals, guide instruction, as well as monitor progress (Sundberg & Partington, 1998; Sundberg & Michael, 2001).

7. Use modeling and prompting with all potential communicative partners in the child's environment.

8. Facilitate generalization by using Stokes & Baer's (1977) strategies for promoting generalization to teach a fully natural language repertoire. For example, teach in the natural environment to facilitate generalization. See a description of Stoke & Baer's strategies under social competence below.

Social Competence

Why Should Social Competence Be a Focus of Intervention?

Difficulty in social and emotional functioning is one of the core defining features of ASD. A major difference between children that are developing typically and children with ASD is the way that they develop social relationships and social skills. From very early on, children will respond to the smiles and eye contact of parents and will naturally reciprocate smiles and eye contact. In contrast, children with ASD do not seem to naturally seek out others socially, read social cues, or demonstrate appropriate social communication. What appears at the core of these social communication deficits is the natural observation and imitation of social skills. Specifically, children with ASD do not appear to seek out social situations or to naturally imitate social skills. For this reason, the focus of intervention to improve these skills relies on teaching these skills through direct instruction, modeling, and specific programming for generalization of skills across settings and people.

What Aspects of Social Competence Should Be Targeted?

A comprehensive social skills package targets the following aspects: a plan to promote skill acquisition, interventions to enhance skill performance, reduction or elimination of any competing problem behaviors, and a plan to facilitate generalization. Therefore, early on in the assessment it is important to not only identify the deficit in skills but why there is a deficit in those skills. Specifically, is it due to a skill deficit, performance deficit, an interfering behavior, or difficulties with generalization of the skill?

The Social Skills Rating System (SSRS) can be utilized to determine specific areas of deficits that should be targeted for remediation as well as identifying strengths that can be used to improve areas of weakness

(Gresham & Elliot, 1990). The SSRS is a rating scale that provides information on the following domains: social skills, including cooperation, empathy, assertion, self-control, and responsibility; as well as a problem behavior; and academic competence. These ratings provide detailed information to inform intervention development.

While some aspects of social functioning may seem subtle and abstract, it is important to establish concrete, specific, measurable goals and behavioral definitions of the social skills identified to guide intervention. As with many of the other aspects of intervention in ASD, early intervention in social functioning is preferred. However, at times deficits in social skills are not usually identified until a child is older, and developmentally there becomes a more pronounced difference between the social competence of the child and his or her peers. Effective interventions for social competence focus on teaching and reinforcing social skills and functioning. These approaches to social skills include the use of prompting, reinforcement, modeling (live or video), and peer-mediated interventions (National Autism Center, 2015; Wang & Parilla, 2011).

How Is Social Competence Improved?

A comprehensive social skills package typically includes the use of explicit instruction of skills through prompting and modeling of specific skills. Some broad areas of consideration for intervention can include: turn-taking, initiating conversation, maintaining conversation, sharing, identifying and understanding of own emotions, as well as the emotions of others, rules of social conduct and nonverbal behavior and meaning. Typically, with social skills instruction, a learner should be provided with the exact information of what to do in given social situations, in clear, concrete language and with pictures or visual cues if necessary. The same can be provided when targeting emotions. Pictures of facial expressions attached to emotions, or picture stories encouraging children to identify the emotions of others can be effective in teaching emotion recognition (Harms, Martin, & Wallace, 2010).

Modeling and video modeling are widely used and have demonstrated effectiveness in teaching social skills (National Autism Center, 2015;

Wang & Parilla, 2011). Live modeling involves a person demonstrating the skill that needs to be imitated in front of the child, and with video modeling, the child is watching a recording of a person demonstrating that skill. If a child has an affinity for computers, then it may be beneficial to use video modeling, since the computer may be a preferred item to the child. Certain characteristics of models make it more likely that the child will imitate. Specifically, the model should be someone that is similar to the child and that the child likes. Remember, much of the reason that children with ASD have deficits in social skills is because they do not appear to naturally imitate others. For this reason, it is essential to specifically point out the aspects of the model's behavior that the child should imitate and the effect that behavior has on the environment. When the child engages in attempts at the target behavior, reinforcement should be provided as well as performance feedback on what went well, what may not have gone well, and what could be done differently next time.

Similar to modeling, peer-training approaches involve the same core principles of prompting, explicit instruction, and reinforcement, but involve training peers to support the social interaction of a child with ASD. Involving peers is beneficial for many reasons, perhaps most importantly for generalization of skills. Peer-training approaches typically occur in the natural environment and during times that are motivating to the learner. Essential procedures in peer-training approaches include effectively training the peer on how to support the intervention, having a peer that is motivated to perform the task, and then reinforcing the peer for engaging in the intervention. Research has shown peer-mediated interventions to be effective with both younger children and older children in improving initiation of conversation as well as assertiveness (Bambara et al., 2016; Chang & Locke, 2016).

In addition to peer-training approaches, Pivotal Response Training (PRT) is an effective intervention for improving specific aspects of social skills related to initiation and responding to social cues. Implementation of PRT works well in the teaching of social skills as the goal is to enhance the motivating aspects of social communication, to train social communication in a natural setting, and to improve initiation of social interaction rather than prompted communication. This is achieved through altering the environment to increase motivation by increasing choice of what to learn, providing social learning situations that are "natural," and reinforcing attempts at social communication (National Autism Center, 2015). Take for example a child that is having difficulty engaging with peers while in the cafeteria. Aspects of PRT, NET, and peer training can be used to help improve this skill through the use of items that are motivating (the child's favorite lunch), while in the natural environment (the cafeteria), involving a peer that is trained on how to respond to attempts to communicate, and reinforcing attempts at social communication by the child.

Cognitive Behavior Interventions (CBIs) involve helping a child identify their thoughts and the feelings associated with those thoughts. For example, a child may avoid social situations because they think, "I will say something and they will laugh at me," and this thought may be paired with fear over initiating social interactions. However, once the thought and the emotion paired with it is identified, then behavioral strategies can be put into place to challenge maladaptive thoughts and the feelings that accompany them. CBIs have shown effectiveness in helping children with adequate receptive and expressive language skills in the understanding of emotional states in themselves, as well as the emotional states in others. Additionally, CBIs can be effective in the promotion of social problem solving, as well as addressing some aspects of social avoidance that may occur as a result of social anxiety (Otero et al., 2015).

While deficits in social competence may be primarily due to a lack of skills in social interaction, they can also be secondary to other core features related to communication, repetitive behaviors, and sensory concerns. Aspects of communication difficulty that may impact social functioning can include delays in spoken language, receptive language, comprehension, as well as stereotyped or repetitive use of language. Social functioning concerns related to stereotyped behavior can include intense preoccupation with special interest, inflexible adherence to routines, repetitive motor mannerisms, and intense rule governed behavior. Each of these concerns can have an impact on social competence, therefore a comprehensive approach to each of the core diagnostic criteria in ASD (social, communication, and repetitive behavior) should be addressed when attempting to improve social competence.

Where and with Whom Should Social Competence Be Addressed?

Essential to social competence is the initiation of skills in the natural environment. For this reason, it is important to consider aspects that will facilitate generalization to the natural environment. Specific aspects of generalization programming should be kept in mind throughout the teaching of social skills and promotion of social competence (Stokes & Baer, 1977). These include:

- Aiming for natural contingencies, specifically, learning is better when it is relevant to the learner and reinforced naturally. In short, try to be as natural as possible during the teaching of social skills.
- Teach multiple examples, highlighting multiple scenarios across settings and people to help promote generalization.
- Focus on self-monitoring skills. This will help students monitor their own skills and behavior without a third party providing observational feedback on their behavior.
- Reinforce moments of generalization.
- Following initial acquisition of the skill, use intermittent and indiscriminable schedules of reinforcement, so that reinforcement is unpredictable.
- Program stimuli common to the natural environment (generalization setting) into the teaching environment by teaching in the natural environment or using the same materials, peers, and so on.
- When teaching vary any stimuli not directly relevant to the teaching strategy or skill itself such as varying conversation topics, varying conversation partners, and so on.

The promotion of social competence and emotional functioning is multifaceted and should be approached from multiple angles depending on the primary cause of the difficulty. It is essential to determine what is contributing to the deficits in social competence (e.g., skill deficit, performance deficit, lack of generalization, social anxiety, lack of social problem-solving skills, difficulty understanding emotions) and to design an intervention that focuses on skill acquisition, enhancing skill performance, reducing interfering behaviors and avoidance, and promoting generalization.

Functional Daily Living Skills

Functional living skills such as dressing, grooming, household chores, and others can be complex skills to learn for children with ASD. These skills usually involve multiple steps and require many prerequisite skills to be successful. Due to the complexity of the skills and the learning needs of children with ASD, these skills often require careful planning and systematic intervention to acquire.

What Are Functional Daily Living Skills?

Many of these skills require a sequence of related skills, known as a behavior or response chain. This chain of responses is related in that each step sets the occasion for the next and reinforces the step prior. In most behavior chains, the steps must occur in a particular sequence in a fluent and sometimes rapid manner. Examples of these multistep skills or behavior chains include: taking a shower, washing hands, getting dressed, making a bed, and making a sandwich.

Why Are Functional Daily Living Skills Important to Teach to Children with ASD?

Many typically developing children learn these types of skills with little to no direct teaching. However, perhaps due to the difficulty in learning from modeling, incidental teaching, and vocal instruction, children with ASD often require explicit and systematic instruction for these skills. Due to the complex, and multistep nature of these types of skills, and the fact that they are typically behaviors performed outside the classroom, they are often more difficult to teach systematically. This is especially true given that children with ASD often need a great deal of repeated practice to learn difficult skills and these behavior chains happen infrequently throughout the day.

Where and When Are Functional Daily Living Skills Taught?

Functional daily living skills occur in all sorts of various locations, mostly outside of the formal classroom. Dressing and grooming skills usually take place in the bedroom or bathroom. Most hygiene skills occur in the bathroom, and many chores happen in rooms throughout the home. Food preparation occurs in the kitchen. These types of settings are not quite set up and organized for structured teaching as a classroom may be. Nevertheless, if the goal is for skills to be demonstrated in these settings, these are the best places for instruction. If functional daily living skills are taught in contrived classroom settings (e.g., teaching tooth brushing at a bowl on a desk in the classroom), the skills are less likely to generalize to the proper setting (e.g., the bathroom sink) where the skills will be expected to occur. This makes it crucial to program for generalization by incorporating strategies such as those described by Stokes and Baer (1977) summarized above in the social competence section. Therefore, it is important to teach the skills in the settings in which they will occur, while also varying your materials (e.g., different types of tooth pastes, tooth brushes, and sinks) so that the skills will generalize to other similar settings (novel sinks). For example, when teaching handwashing, teach in a bathroom sink, but use different types of sinks, paper towels, soaps, and so on during the course of instruction, so that the learner will be able to wash their hands in any type of sink they may encounter.

How Are Functional Daily Living Skills Taught?

The first step in teaching a functional daily living skill is to break the complex behavior chain into all of its component steps. This is called developing a task analysis. The best ways to develop a task analysis are to observe someone completing the task or to complete the task yourself, and write down each step as it is completed. The number of steps involved in the task analysis will depend on the skills the learner already displays.

Following are two examples of task analyses for showering. The simple task analysis could be used for a learner who is able to display the behaviors within each step. For example, within Step 4, a learner should be able to wet hair, open shampoo, squeeze shampoo into hand, lather hair, rinse hair, and so on. For an individual that is still learning to do these steps, they may need a more detailed task analysis such as the complex task analysis in the right side of the column may be needed.

Simple task analysis	Complex task analysis
1. Start shower	1. Start water
2. Remove clothes	2. Adjust water temperature
3. Get into shower	3. Divert water to shower head
4. Wash hair	4. Remove clothes
5. Wash face	5. Step into shower
6. Wash Arms, chest, stomach, and back	6. Wet hair
7. Wash genitals	7. Open shampoo bottle
8. Wash legs and feet	8. Squeeze quarter size shampoo dollop onto hand
9. Rinse	9. Put shampoo onto hair and lather
10. Turn off water	10. Rinse hair
11. Dry off	11. Open face wash
12. Step out of shower	12. Squeeze dime size face wash dollop into hand

Developing a task analysis may seem quite simple, but can sometimes involve quite a bit of initial assessment of the learner as well as researching the various ways to complete a complex skill. For example, some people wash their face before washing their hair in the shower. Although, either method or sequence may be acceptable, an instructor should select one for the task analysis to be consistent in teaching the learner. Otherwise acquisition of the skill may be delayed.

Once the task analysis is developed for the skill, a baseline assessment should be conducted to determine which steps in the task analysis, if any, the learner can already display. For example, a child may be able to rub their face, but not get face wash, wash their face, and rinse. Or they may be able to shampoo their hair, but not wash their legs. Taking this type of baseline data is quick and easy and will help the instructor determine which teaching method will be most efficient and which steps to focus on during teaching. To take this type of baseline data, a data sheet should be developed with each step in the task analysis and a space for a + or − to record if the learner did the step or was not able to do the step independently. To conduct the assessment, give the learner the initial instruction such as, "take a shower," and give a set period of time to initiate the task (e.g., 30 seconds). If the first step is not completed within that time frame, record a − and then complete the step out of their view if possible. If the first step is completed by the learner independently, record a +. Once that first step is complete, allow them a chance to do the second step. If that second step is completed by the learner independently, record a +. If the second step is not completed by the learner, complete the step out of view and record a −. Once the second step is completed, allow time to complete the third step. Continue this process through all the steps so that the learner is given the opportunity to display each step, even if they could not do the one before. Once the assessment is completed, calculate a percentage of steps completed independently and review the data sheet to determine if the steps that need instruction are toward the beginning of the task analysis, the end, or are spread throughout.

There are three main common methods of teaching task analyses: forward chaining, backward chaining, and total task presentation. Forward chaining refers to teaching the first step of the task analysis using most-to-least prompting or errorless teaching, while either fully prompting the rest of the steps or completing them for the learner. This allows the learner to work on one step at a time, while still completing the entire chain each teaching session to maintain the links between the steps. For example, in the first session of forward chaining, most-to-least prompting or errorless teaching is initiated on the first step first. The instructor provides hand-over-hand prompting, or the most physical prompting necessary, for the learner to complete the first step successfully, and then provides physical prompting through the rest of the steps. During the second session, prompts are typically faded from the first teaching step (e.g., the instructor may use partial physical prompts), so that the learner starts to become independent on that step, while the instructor then physically prompts or completes the rest of the task analysis for them. The instructor will continue fading the prompts at the first step, while still physically prompting through the remaining steps until the learner is completely independent with the first step. Then the learner will complete the first step independently and the instructor will start to fade the prompts on the second step while physically prompting the remaining steps to the end. This will continue, step by step, until the learner is independent with every step in the task analysis. This teaching method allows the learner to do a little bit of work in the beginning of the task, but gets lots of help completing the rest of the task until the steps are learned.

Backward chaining involves teaching the last step in the task analysis first. For example, the instructor will physically prompt the learner through Steps 1 to 9 in a 10-step chain and start to fade out the prompts on Step 10 in the first few teaching sessions. Then once the learner is able to complete Step 10 independently, the instructor will complete Steps 1 to 8 using physical prompting, fade out the prompts on Step 9, and allow the learner to complete Step 10 independently. This will continue until the learner can complete all the steps independently. This teaching method allows the learner to get help through the first part of the task analysis, and then do just a little bit of work at the end, right before a reinforcer is delivered.

The total task presentation method requires teaching at every step in the task analysis during every session. For each step, the instructor allows the learner an opportunity to perform the step. If they are not able to perform the step, the instructor provides least-to-most prompting at each step. For example, during each teaching session of a 10-step task analysis, the instructor would start by giving an instruction to complete the task. If the learner does not start the task within a few seconds, the instructor will provide a verbal or gestural prompt. If they still do not start the task, the instructor may provide a partial physical prompt. If they still do not start the task, the instructor may provide a full physical prompt and then wait for the learner to start the second step. If they do not start the second step, the instructor will give a verbal or gestural prompt for the second step. If the learner does not start the second step at this point, the instructor will give a partial physical prompt. If the learner still does not start the second step, the instructor will provide a full physical prompt and then wait for the learner to start the third step. This will continue until the task is completed. This teaching method allows the learner an opportunity to complete each step independently before getting help, during each teaching session.

Choosing the chaining instructional method that is appropriate for the learner depends on a variety of different factors. There is no definitive research that indicates that one method (i.e., forward chaining, backward chaining, or total task presentation) is more effective or efficient than the other for all learners. However, conceptually there are some factors that may lead an instructor to choose one over the other in a given situation. Specifically, if a learner demonstrates many of the first few steps independently in the task analysis (but not the steps at the end of the task analysis) during baseline, then it might be efficient to teach the behavior chain using forward chaining. Similarly, if the learner demonstrates many of the last few steps independently of the task analysis (but not the steps at the beginning of the task), then backwards chaining might be more efficient. Alternatively, if during baseline, the learner independently demonstrates steps scattered throughout the task analysis, then teaching using total task presentation might be more economical. It also may be true that some students may learn more effectively using one method and others another. Also, for individuals who are at a lower level of functioning, backwards chaining may be more effective since the hardest work for the learner is at the end of the task immediately before a reinforcer or a break.

Strategies for promoting generalization and maintenance should be incorporated into any instruction on functional skills to ensure that the skills will be demonstrated in all the appropriate settings and situations. For example, it is important to ensure after teaching a child to wash clothes that they can wash clothes in any washing machine they encounter. Or, if a child is taught to reply to the question, "How are you?" they should reply with various responses, not just the, "I'm fine," phrase they were taught, but, "good," "great," and so on. Strategies for promoting generalization include teaching multiple exemplars, ensuring natural contingencies of reinforcement are presented, teaching settings sequentially, varying irrelevant stimuli during instruction, using common stimuli between the instructional and generalization settings, using delayed and intermittent reinforcement, using self-management strategies, and reinforcing novel responses (Stokes & Baer, 1977).

Regardless of the instructional method chosen, it is critical that data are collected prior to teaching and during each teaching session to determine how quickly progress is being made. Using a data sheet (described earlier) with each step in the task analysis and a space to document if the step was performed independently, correctly or incorrectly, and with prompting is an easy way to track progress. The data collected should be evaluated after each session and graphed to determine if changes to the instructional strategy should be considered.

Academic Intervention

Best practices in academic programming for children with ASD tend to be similar to best practices for all children. The primary deficits in ASD typically surround social functioning and language or communication, while academic functioning can be within the normal range. When assessing the academic programming of any child, it is important to assess the child's progress on the skills being reviewed in the curriculum and the progress made toward those goals. A determination for additional programming should be made based on whether or not a learner is meeting the academic goals of the curriculum, or if there are behaviors that impede learning. If a determination is made that there are behaviors that impede learning, such as disruptive or repetitive behavior, then a decision should be made on what accommodations and specially designed instruction should be provided.

Areas to consider when evaluating the academic structure for all students including children with ASD involve the instructional practices, the curriculum, the learning environment, and individual characteristics of the learner (Hops, 2008). Interventions and accommodations are based on these aspects of the learning system. Specifically, the instruction and curriculum involve the information that is being taught to the student and how this information is being taught. Likewise, consideration of aspects of the learning environment as well as individual characteristics of the student should be considered.

What Academic Skills Are Taught?

When programming for a child with ASD, it is important to match the curriculum to the instructional goals of the child. If a child is making appropriate gains within the general curriculum, then the actual content may not need to be changed. If this is the case, then specific modifications or accommodations can be made to the curriculum if needed. Some examples of accommodations can include limiting the amount of information that is presented at once, or modifying exams and how the skills presented in the curriculum are assessed. However, if a child is not making progress with the general curriculum, then specific changes to the curriculum based on the individual goals of the child should be made. The best instructional strategy is to match the curriculum to the skill level of the child. If you look at skills from a continuum of mastery to instructional and then frustrational, a child should be instructed at his or her instructional level. If it is determined that individualized instruction is needed then assessments such as Assessment of Basic Language and Learning Skills-Revised (ABLLS-R) or Verbal Behavior Milestones Assessment and Placement Program (VB-MAPP) can be initiated (Partington, 2006; Sundberg, 2008). These two assessments provide current levels of functioning on a variety of skills (including academic) and can be used to establish and monitor progress on individualized goals.

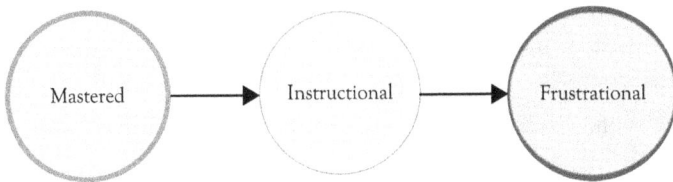

How Should Academic Programming Be Provided?

Aspects of instruction involve how the curriculum is relayed to students. There are many ways to provide content to children within the classroom including: lectures, demonstrations, role play, discussions, modeling, and so on. Characteristics inherent in the diagnostic criteria of ASD and potentially identified as areas of weakness in the ABLLS or VB-MAPP should also be targeted for intervention. In addition to academic skills such as reading, writing, and Math, additional skills specific to ASD may include academic readiness and language skills. Some widely implemented instructional strategies that have demonstrated effectiveness in the literature include: prompting sequences, errorless teaching procedures, discrete trial training, explicit instruction, and natural environment training (Smith, 2001; National Autism Center, 2015).

Prompting Sequences and Errorless Teaching

Prompts are ways to provide assistance in guiding children to the correct response during instruction. A prompt is given (usually by the instructor) between a cue (or instruction) and the student's response. Prompting sequences are often termed least-to-most or most-to-least prompting depending on the amount of assistance provided and when it is delivered. In a least-to-most prompting sequence, a child is provided with an instruction or cue (e.g., instruction to "touch blue" given an array of color cards), the instructor will then wait for a response, and if after a specified wait time, the child does not respond (wait times should vary based on the individual learning needs of the child), then the child will be prompted with a least intrusive prompt such as a gesture (e.g., touch blue while the instructor points to blue), again the instructor will wait for a response, and if no response then the instructor may provide light physical guidance at the elbow or wrist. If the child still does not respond, the instructor may move to hand-over-hand guidance to touch blue. Similar least-to-most prompt hierarchies could be created for nonphysical skills as well, such as in verbal language.

Most-to-least prompting strategies, also called errorless teaching, are strategies in which the instructor provides scaffolded assistance that is faded out systematically. For example, for physical skills, a prompt hierarchy beginning with hand-over-hand guidance may be used and then faded over time as the child becomes more independent with the skill. Using the receptive identification example provided earlier, an instructor may cue the child to "touch blue" and immediately provide hand-over-hand assistance. On the next trial (or session, depending on criteria set by the instructor), the instructor may begin to fade the prompts by saying, "touch blue" and then immediately provide a light physical prompt at the elbow. After the child is successful at this prompt level for a given period of time (criteria set by the instructor), the instructor may then begin using gestural prompts. This continues until the prompt is completely faded and the child independently completes the skill. Most-to-least prompting can also be performed for nonphysical skills such as in verbal language instruction.

Another prompt hierarchy that can be used following a most-to-least or errorless teaching design is time-delay prompts. In this procedure, one type of prompt is selected (e.g., verbal or gestural) and is provided immediately after the cue and then faded by delaying the prompt over successive trials or sessions. For example, to teach a response of "blue" to the instruction of "What color is this?" the teacher may begin instruction by saying, "What color is this? Blue." Then over time they would insert a delay between the instruction and the prompt. This might look like saying, "What color is this?" waiting 5 seconds, then saying, "Blue." This prompt delay is increased as the child says the correct answer before the prompt is given. Alternatively, the time delay may be inserted on the first trial and held constant throughout instruction. This is a called a constant time delay procedure and is contrasted with the progressive time delay procedure described above.

Discrete Trial Training (DTT)

DTT (also called Discrete Trial Instruction or DTI) has become almost synonymous with ASD teaching approaches and applied behavior analysis. While DTT has been shown to be one of the most effective approaches to teaching certain skills to a child with ASD, it should be noted that it is not the only strategy and certainly not a panacea. Discrete trial-training involves explicit instruction to teach a particular skill which includes five parts: cue, prompt, response, consequence, and inter-trial interval (Smith, 2001). Discrete trial training can be used to teach any type of skill that can be broken down into discrete, measurable units (e.g., labeling items, Math facts). Manualized instructions for developing instructional programs for children with ASD using discrete trial training are readily available (e.g., Maurice, Green, & Luce, 1996). For example, take a child that is learning colors. In the cue section, the instructor would present a clear directive "What color is that?" This can also include a prompt to assist in responding (as described in the section above). Next the child will respond (pick a color). In the consequence stage the child will be provided with a reinforcer for the correct response or some type of error correction following an incorrect response. Then after a brief delay, the next trial begins. Trials are presented in a fast pace in either massed format or interspersed with already mastered skills to facilitate many opportunities for practice. DTT has benefits in children with ASD, since due to difficulties with social awareness and communication, children with ASD do not always naturally pick up instruction or attend without structured and systematic support. In fact, using DTT and other aspects of applied behavior analysis, Lovaas (1987) was able to teach fundamental skills and decrease challenging behavior in children with ASD to such an extent that they were indistinguishable from their typically developing same-aged peers when entering school. However, it is crucial that DTT is used for appropriate skills, and that attempts are made to make DTT enjoyable and something the child wants to do, as sometimes DTT can evoke problem behavior (Shillingsburg, Bowen, & Shapiro, 2014) if used without other strategies of applied behavior analysis.

Explicit Instruction

Explicit instruction refers to instruction in which skills are broken down and taught using a scaffolded assistance design. This is different from other techniques where the child is guided or allowed to learn through exploratory activities. Instead, the child is directly taught skills that are lacking. An example of an explicit instruction is Direct Instruction (DI) which is a scripted curriculum utilizing carefully designed instructional strategies, active student responding, and guided practice to teach areas such as Math and Reading (Englemann & Carnine, 1982). There are DI curricula materials commercially available and these are becoming more and more common in school district initiatives as research shows they can advance students graded levels within one academic year. Explicit instruction typically involves some of the methods already described above (e.g., prompting sequences and DTT).

Naturalistic Teaching Strategies

In contrast to DTT, but potentially as effective when used appropriately, are naturalistic teaching strategies (NTS), sometimes referred to as incidental teaching or NET (Natural Environment Teaching). NTS involves using materials that naturally occur in the environment to teach skills across multiple setting and activities. NTS is "child directed" with a focus on teaching with activities, items, and methods that are motivating to the child and using consequences that naturally occur in the environment. Overall effective teaching strategies such as DI, modeling, prompting, and errorless teaching can be used as part of NTS. This method has documented effectiveness in the literature and is effective for increasing motivation to learn skills as well as promoting the generalization of skills across people, settings, and different activities (National Autism Center, 2015).

Where Should Academic Instruction Occur?

Aspects of the environment related to student learning include not only the physical aspects, but also the rules and expectations, the relationship between teacher and student, and the approach to discipline in relation to which behaviors are reinforced in the environment. Things to observe in the physical environment that may impact learning include the placement of chairs and desks, if the environment is physically distracting, the temperature and lighting, and if there are designated areas for particular activities (Hops, 2008). Additionally, instructors should take note of the rules and routines of the classroom such as posting and explicitly teaching expectations, the ratio of positive versus corrective language in the classroom, and creating specific routines for work completion, transitions, and "down time." Classrooms should be purposefully designed to enhance independent responding and learning. This could include increasing the likelihood of requiring communication by requesting needed items that are out of reach, arranging materials and group areas to encourage cooperative learning, keeping instructional materials neat and organized for easy access, as well as other strategies. Culture in the classroom linked to positive academic outcomes includes fostering an environment that reinforces learning and effort, which focuses on building relationships and promoting positive interactions between adults and peers.

What Individual Learner Needs Should Be Considered?

An essential aspect of the instructional environment is the match between the environment and the learner. Observing the individual needs of a student as well as individual strengths and weaknesses may help determine why a student may be struggling in the environment. Say for example, a child has a weakness in verbal skills and the majority of instruction is presented verbally. This would present a mismatch between the instructional approach and the individual characteristics of the child. Changing the instructional approach to increase the focus on the incorporation of more visual supports would provide a better match between the environment and learner.

As part of the Individuals with Disabilities Education Act (IDEA), all children are entitled to a free and appropriate public education (FAPE) in the Least Restrictive Environment (LRE) (34 C.F.R. §300.550). LRE entitles children to receive their education in the environment that they would have if they were not classified with a disability. This is typically their neighborhood school in a regular education classroom. For this reason, every attempt should be made to educate children with and without ASD in a regular education classroom with their peers, and with an Individualized Education Plan (IEP) if necessary. If a child is not making progress because he or she requires additional supports that cannot be provided in the regular education classroom, then pull out services (receiving services outside of the classroom such as speech therapy or occupational therapy) can be initiated. Additionally, if the individual needs of a child require that he or she be placed in a class that is different from the regular education classroom, then attempts at mainstreaming should be made when possible such as during lunch, recess, and physical education. An even more restrictive setting, such as a special education school, may be required for severe needs. Educating a child in the LRE is a delicate balance between the individual needs of the child and the structure of the classroom to promote meaningful educational benefit.

Transition and Vocational Programming

Why Should Transition and Vocational Skill Programming Be Included in the Educational Programming for a Child with ASD?

The characteristics of ASD do not change drastically when a child turns 21. However, the funding for services that most states and local counties provide a child with ASD drastically decreases, as do the options for quality service providers. At age 21, most states are no longer required to provide educational services through the local school district. However, many counties or townships are able to provide funding for adult services such as day programs, supported employment, and residential settings. Of note, these types of programs often have much less structured supports and less educational focus, as well as lack age-appropriate programming for adults. These barriers compounded with the fact that many underfunded adult programs do not have the resources to treat adults with ASD who may engage in challenging or problem behavior, make it difficult for adults to find placements in which they can be successful.

As a result, it is crucial that educational programming focus on transitioning children with ASD to less structured support from an early age to foster more independence and success in adult settings. In fact, the IDEA requires that transitioning programming starts in the Individualized Education Plan (IEP) at age 16 (20 USC §1400 et seq). Many states require that it starts earlier (e.g., age 14) and best practice would suggest that programming should always look toward the child's long-term goals.

Who Is Responsible for Transition and Vocational Programming for a Child with ASD?

Ultimately it is the teacher's responsibility, along with the student's multidisciplinary team of professionals, to include transitional and vocational programming for any child over the age of 16 into the IEP (and earlier in some states). However, teachers should be considering the goals of the student post age 21 from a much earlier educational age, even though it is not required by law. Teachers can do this simply by selecting more functional goals to target during instruction. Transitional programming is sometimes not as structured as academic programming, and often is not an area of great focus in preservice teacher education programs. Due to this, teachers may be less prepared to suggest, develop, or implement transitional or vocational programming with their students.

Parents can also contribute to transitional programming by suggesting areas to target, as well as contribute to discussions about long-term goals for residential settings and secondary education or vocational placements. Parents know their children best and may be the best team member to suggest preferences and hobbies that could be related to vocational placements. For example, a child that likes to sort and manipulate paper, may be happy and successful in a clerical vocational setting. Perhaps most importantly, adolescents should also be involved as an active member of their transition planning and establishing goals for the future (Hendricks & Wheman, 2009). It is important that parents become educated about the day and residential options available to them well before age 16. This helps to ensure they fulfill any prerequisite requirements for funding, as well as engage in effective and frequent advocacy for their child. Accessing information about these options and funding may be difficult in some areas as resources for adults are often not as well organized as school services at the federal, state, or local level. To promote successful transition planning every member of the team including the adolescent, teachers, parents, speech pathologists, teachers' assistants, occupational therapists, physical therapists, school psychologists, and anyone involved in the child's programming should constantly be looking toward the child's long-term goals while developing programming.

What Should Transition and Vocational Programming Include?

Transitional and vocational programming should prepare the adolescent with ASD to be successful in the adult placement (both day and residential) in which they will eventually enroll. These settings can be very different from the school settings that students experience prior to turning age 21. Often in these settings there is less supervision. Staff to student ratios typically go from 1:1 or 1:2 in a special educational setting to 1:6 or 1:8 in an adult setting. Often, due to these ratios and lack of funding and resources, adults with ASD in day programs may be left unengaged for long periods of time which may result in a regression of skills and challenging behaviors. Also, less supervision results in less support performing functional living skills such as hygiene and meal preparation (Paone & Meyer, 2009).

Due to the differences between the settings a child with ASD experiences and the settings an adult with ASD experiences, transitional programming in the educational environment should focus on teaching skills that will allow the adult with ASD to be as independent as possible. Goals for transitional programming should include: academics that are functional (e.g., reading signs, menus), daily living skills (e.g., toileting, dressing), independent travel (e.g., walking down hallways, streets, using public transportation), social skills (e.g., reading social cues, asking for help, using polite greetings), reducing challenging behavior (e.g., yelling, stereotypy), home skills (e.g., cleaning, cooking), and teaching appropriate leisure skills (e.g., activities that can be done independently that the child enjoys). Any goals selected should be assessed to ensure they are important for the child's future (e.g., will the skill be used 10 years from now?). As the child ages, the goals should shift from more academic skills (e.g., reading "cat," recalling multiplication facts) to more functional skills (e.g., reading common community sight words, using a calculator).

Vocational goals should be selected based on the likely postsecondary placement for the student. This should be determined based on the student's skills and interests. For example, if the student has interests in computers, perhaps a vocational position incorporating computer use could be selected such as computer programming or secretarial work. If these vocations are future placements, then skills such as navigating computer applications could be taught. If the student likes to disassemble machines, a vocational position might include disassembling electronics for recycling programs. For this vocation, skills such as using a screw driver and sorting parts could be taught.

When goals are selected they should be written in measurable terms with practical and achievable criteria. Goals should be functional for long-term benefit, achievable yet challenging, age appropriate, and based on interests and needs. For example, a leisure skill goal could be worded as remaining seated for 10 minutes while independently completing an age-appropriate puzzle without any prompts from adults or caregivers. The goal should be achievable and may not always end in complete independence. For example, perhaps a child needs help getting the puzzle and setting it up, but can then sit independently. Instruction should focus on making sure the student has everything they need to be as independent as possible. A report in 2015 found that 37 percent of individuals with ASD were "disconnected" at age 20, meaning they never got a job or continued their education (Roux et al., 2015). The choice of appropriate goals is crucial because lack of addressing independence in many of these areas could result in physical harm, potential for neglect or abuse, more restrictive placements, and unhappiness.

Where Should Transition and Vocational Programming Occur?

Transitional programming should first include an assessment of the child's preferences, skills, and family structure to create a realistic vision of the long-term placement options for the student. Living options may include family home, group home, foster home, apartment living, or supported living. Postsecondary options for children with ASD may include college, competitive employment, supported employment, or day programs. Supported employment options may be in the form of a small business enterprise, mobile work crew, enclave, an individualized employment setting, or a sheltered workshop.

Once the team determines the most likely postsecondary placements for the child, they can then include similar settings in the transitional programming. Programming could start by teaching any prerequisite skills in the classroom and then teach and practice the vocational and transitional skills selected in the community setting where the skills will most likely take place. This may include job settings such as grocery stores, clerical offices, community colleges or 4-year colleges and universities. Instruction in the community is often called community-based instruction and is crucial to ensuring success in the future placements.

When Should Transition and Vocational Programming Begin?

IDEA requires that an Individualized Transition Plan (ITP) be developed for children ages 16 and older. Some states require this begins at 14 or even earlier. Ultimately, transition and vocational programming should be started as early as possible, including from the very beginning of any formal education, especially in long-term planning and goal selection. The ITP should include postsecondary goals that are based on age-appropriate transition assessments and should be related to education and training for future employment and living settings.

How Should Transition and Vocational Programming Be Conducted?

IDEA also defines transition services as activities that are results-oriented, facilitates the transition from school to postsecondary placements, is based on the needs, strengths, and preferences of the child, and includes instruction, related services, community instruction, employment and daily living skills as appropriate (34 C.F.R. §300.348). Transitional programming should abide by some common guiding principles that include programming in the LRE, preference-based teaching, person-centered planning, enhancing quality of life, evidence-based practices, and presuming the highest level of skills and intellect.

Prior to starting transitional and vocational programming, the child's current skill level should be assessed and goals should be developed based on achievable criteria. Some general assessments exist for this purpose such as the Vineland (Sparrow, Cichetti, & Saulnier, 2016); Assessment of Functional Living Skills (AFLS; Partington and Mueller, 2012); and the Reading Free Vocational Interest Inventory (Becker, 2001). In addition, individualized vocational situational assessments can be conducted in which an instructor exposes a child to different vocational settings and tasks and collects data on their skill level and indicators of preference. The Vineland and AFLS also have sections on functional daily living skills to determine current skill level in those areas.

Once the current skill levels are determined for both transitional and vocational skills and goals are selected and written, instruction can begin. Instruction should be individualized to the skill being taught and to the individual child's learning history. A teaching program can be developed for each skill using the most appropriate instructional strategy, many of which have been described in previous sections of this text. Instructional strategies can include behavioral chaining, shaping, discrete trial instruction, modeling, and appropriate prompt hierarchies.

Some common instructional strategies used for transitional and vocational skills include video-based instruction such as video modeling or video prompting, and behavioral skills training. Video modeling involves showing the learner a video of a task and then asking the learner to perform the skills immediately after viewing. This can be done in the community (e.g., via an iPad or other portable video device) or in classroom settings. Research has used video modeling to teach a variety of skills from social, communicative skills to vocational skills (Delano, 2007; McCoy & Hermansen, 2007; Ayres & Langone, 2005). Video prompting is a variation of video modeling in which the skills are broken into various brief video clips and the learner is asked to watch one clip and perform the first step of that task and then watch the next clip to perform the next step and so on. Video prompting has been used to teach domestic, vocational, and functional living skills effectively (Banda, Dogoe, & Matuszny, 2011).

Behavioral Skills Training (BST) is a package instructional strategy used to teach complex skills. The strategy starts with a description (e.g., written and verbal) of the skill to be performed. The skills are then modeled by the instructor. The learner is then provided the opportunity to practice the skill while the instructor delivers feedback (both corrective and supportive). Practice is continued in role play situations until the learner is able to display the skills accurately. Then the skill is demonstrated in the natural environment. BST has been used to teach various social skills and vocational skills effectively to children and adults with ASD (Palmen, Didden, & Korzilius, 2010; Stewart, Carr, & LeBlanc, 2007; Palmen & Didden, 2012; Nuernberger et al., 2013).

Prior to and during instruction, data should be collected to monitor progress on each transitional and vocational goal. The data collection should be individualized and appropriate to the skill as defined in the goal. Data collection should include direct observation of the skill and could be in the form of frequency, duration, latency, and so on, depending on the most important dimension of the behavior targeted. For example, data collection may include the number of tasks completed, the length of time engaged, the speed with which a task is completed, and accuracy of a skill or task. Data should be collected by anyone able to frequently observe the skill targeted and graphed immediately to display trends so that decisions can be made quickly in regards to changes in instructional strategy.

As described previously, the location of instruction should match the setting in which the skills will ultimately be performed. Community-based instruction helps to ensure that skills learned will generalize to the settings and situations in which the child will ultimately need to display the skills (Kluth, 2000). For example, using hands-on teaching of daily living skills in the home, and vocational skills in the work setting will make the instruction more relevant and allow the instructor to embed more natural reinforcers that will maintain the target skill in the long term. Instruction on skills could be first taught in a classroom setting to ensure errorless teaching in a more contrived setting, and then moved into the community for generalization (e.g., Browder, Snell, & Wildonger, 1988). Community-based instruction will have its challenges, but can be successfully implemented if a plan is developed that incorporates how opportunities will be presented, how reinforcement will be delivered, and how challenging behaviors will be handled if they occur. The plan should include evidence-based instructional strategies and practical data collection as well. A back-up for community instruction is always a good idea in case the unexpected occurs (e.g., transportation issues, closed community sites, or challenging behavior). Role play activities used in contrived settings to preteach skills can be beneficial as well as using visual aids and reminders. Using self-management interventions such as self-monitoring (having the learner collect data on the accuracy of their skills), self-evaluation (having the learner evaluate the accuracy of their performance as compared to some criteria), and reminders in the form of visual cues and devices can be very effective and allow the instructor to fade easily from the setting. Technology is also a useful tool in community-based instruction. Technology such as Bluetooth communication can be used to discretely prompt the learner in the community and iPads or other personal devices can include activity schedules, reminders, and video-based instruction that can be used independently by the learner (Graves et al., 2005; Allen et al., 2010, Wehman, 2012; Gentry et al., 2010; Goldsmith & LeBlanc, 2004).

Function-Based Interventions for Challenging Behavior

Interventions for problem behaviors displayed by children with ASD should be based on ecologically appropriate functional behavioral assessments (FBAs). Once an FBA is completed, a clinician can proceed through the problem-solving model to develop an intervention that is individualized to the child's environment and learning history. There are a variety of challenging behaviors that a child with ASD may display. These could range from stereotypy (i.e., repetitive body movements), and scripting (e.g., repeating phrases irrelevant to the situation) to aggression (e.g., hitting, kicking, biting), property destruction (e.g., throwing objects, writing on furniture, breaking objects), or self-injurious behavior (e.g., head banging or head hitting, self-pinching, eye poking). Problem or challenging behaviors could also include more complex issues such as sleep difficulty, food selectivity, or inappropriate sexual behaviors. These types of issues may require some medical testing prior to behavioral intervention to rule out any medical causes and may require the help of a professional consultant. In general, regardless of the challenging behavior, an FBA should first be conducted followed by development of an individualized positive behavior support plan. The ensuing guidelines apply to any challenging behavior targets, although the specific interventions may vary. The reader is encouraged to seek advice from the research literature and training prior to implementing any specific interventions.

Why Is It Important to Link the Assessment to the Intervention?

There are several reasons why the intervention should be directly related to the FBA. First, research has shown that interventions based on an FBA are more effective than those interventions chosen randomly (e.g., Ingram et al., 2005). This allows for efficiency in choosing the intervention that will be most effective first. Second, basing the intervention on the assessment helps the clinician to determine which intervention to select instead of using trial and error which can be frustrating, time consuming, and affect the trust in the clinician's skills by those requesting the intervention. Third, in order to develop an intervention that will be implemented with a high degree of fidelity, it is critical to understand the natural setting and caretakers who will be implementing the intervention. This understanding often comes from the interviews and observations conducted during the FBA. If an intervention is not practical and safe to implement, then it is not likely to be implemented with fidelity, and therefore, not positively affect the target behavior. This could result in wasted time and resources in designing an effective intervention that will not be implemented. For this reason, an intervention needs to not only be effective in changing the behavior, but also be easily implemented and socially acceptable by the caregivers implementing it.

What Does It Mean to Link the Intervention to the FBA?

The product of an FBA is a hypothesis of behavioral function. This allows the subsequent intervention to be based on addressing that function. For an intervention to be function-based, it should: address the relevant antecedent variables that trigger the behavior in order to prevent or minimize the behavior; teach a replacement behavior that serves to allow the child to gain access to the same reinforcer maintaining the problem behavior; and address the consequences maintaining the behavior so that it is less likely to occur (O'Neill et al., 2015).

Who Develops the Intervention Plan?

Ideally, the clinician (e.g., behavior analyst, school psychologist, or behavior consultant) who conducted the FBA should develop the intervention plan in collaboration with other individuals on the child's team. Regardless of the person's title, they should have training in applied behavior analysis, experience in developing similar interventions for children with ASD, and have an intimate knowledge of the child's environment. In addition, the clinician should collaborate with the parents, caregivers, staff, and anyone implementing the intervention or with knowledge or investment in the effectiveness of the intervention. This will increase the likelihood that the intervention will be implemented as it is written and acceptable to those implementing it. Finally, the clinician that developed the intervention should also be the one to train those implementing it to ensure effective implementation.

How Is an Individualized Intervention Developed?

As described above, a function-based intervention plan will include three types of interventions: (a) preventative interventions that address the relevant antecedent variables that trigger the behavior; (b) instructional strategies to teach a replacement behavior that serves to allow the child to gain access to the same reinforcer; and (c) reactive interventions that address the consequences maintaining the behavior so that it is less likely to occur.

Antecedent or "A" Strategies

Preventative strategies (think of them as "A" strategies as they deal with the "antecedents" of the behavior) will usually address the motivation (often called motivating operations) of the child to engage in the target behavior or increase the overall access to the reinforcer. The rationale is to arrange the environment such that there is no need for the child to engage in the problem behavior because the environment is enjoyable, and they get frequent access to the functional reinforcer (this is sometimes referred to as noncontingent reinforcement when the functional reinforcer is systematically delivered on a schedule). For example, suppose that a child's problem behavior of hitting typically occurs when he is given a Math worksheet that is too difficult and he gets a break from the worksheet contingent on hitting. One antecedent intervention could be to modify the worksheet to be more appropriate to his skill level, reduce the length of the assignment, or provide him with help during completion. Another intervention could include giving him frequent breaks during the Math worksheet so that he does not *need* to hit to get access to a break. Likewise, if a child with ASD typically screams when his teacher talks to another child instead of him, and contingent on screaming the teacher reprimands him (i.e., gives attention), what would be appropriate antecedent interventions? Perhaps giving frequent attention by giving him attention when he is quiet. Other antecedent variables that could be modified to help minimize or prevent the problem behavior could include addressing sleep, hunger, and other relevant health issues.

Replacement Behavior or "B" Strategies

Another type of intervention focuses on teaching a replacement behavior (to remember, think of them as "B" strategies since they deal with a target behavior). The rationale for these interventions is to teach a child a more appropriate way to access the same functional reinforcer identified during the FBA. If a child is not taught a more appropriate way to get access to the maintaining reinforcer, then even if the current target behavior is decreased through other interventions, a new problem behavior will likely emerge. For example, in the earlier scenario of a child that engages in problem behavior to escape a difficult Math worksheet, an appropriate replacement behavior may be to teach the child to ask for help or a break. This would get him access to the maintaining reinforcer (escape from difficult work), but in a way that is more appropriate than hitting. If the child is not taught a way to ask for help, even if screaming is decreased, hitting (or another challenging behavior) may emerge. In the second example, what would be an appropriate replacement behavior for a child that screams to access teacher attention? Perhaps appropriate requests for attention, such as raising his or her hand, or asking a question. If these replacement behaviors are not taught but the hitting and screaming are decreased, these children would likely find another inappropriate way to get breaks and attention such as spitting, kicking, or cursing.

A common replacement behavior intervention is called Functional Communication Training (FCT) and involves teaching a functionally equivalent replacement behavior (one that gets the child access to the reinforcer maintaining the problem behavior as found in the FBA), while no longer reinforcing the problem behavior (this is called extinction and will be described in the following section). This intervention was first developed by Carr and Durand in 1985, and many researchers and clinicians since have developed systematic protocols for teaching the replacement communicative response (Wacker et al., 1990; Hagopian et al., 1998; Fisher et al., 1993; Durand, 1999). Other types of interventions that involve teaching appropriate replacement behaviors may include general communication instruction, social skills instruction, compliance training, and schedule following.

Consequence or "C" Strategies

The third type of intervention involves reactions or consequences to the problem behavior. There are three common types of consequence strategies: extinction, differential reinforcement, and punishment. Extinction is the term used when the intervention involves no longer providing the reinforcer that is maintaining the problem behavior (the reinforcer found in the FBA). Extinction could be implemented with positive reinforcers (events or items added to the environment) or negative reinforcers (events or items removed from the environment). In the preceding Math worksheet example, the reinforcer maintaining the hitting is delay or escape from the Math worksheet. This is negative reinforcement (removal of the worksheet maintains the behavior). Extinction would involve ensuring that the child does not escape from completing the worksheet following any challenging behavior, through interventions such as prompting to continue working, and ensuring that the worksheet stays in front of the child. For the preceding second example, screaming is maintained by access to reinforcement which is positive reinforcement. What would extinction look like? Perhaps ensuring the child does not get any attention contingent on screaming. Important to note, extinction is not the same as ignoring. If attention is the reinforcer for the problem behavior, then extinction may look like ignoring the problem behavior. But if the reinforcer is negative reinforcement (e.g., escape from something), then ignoring the behavior might still be allowing the child to escape and thus reinforce the problem behavior further. Also important to note, anytime extinction is used, a replacement behavior should also be taught so that the child learns the appropriate way to access the reinforcer. The effects of extinction often involve the challenging behavior increasing before it decreases—in other words, it may get worse before it gets better. Therefore extinction should be implemented with this in mind and only after consideration of these types of side effects and how they will be handled.

A second type of consequence intervention is called differential reinforcement. Differential reinforcement is a combination of reinforcing a replacement behavior and extinction. FCT is a type of differential reinforcement where an appropriate replacement behavior is reinforced while the problem behavior no longer gains the person access to the reinforcer. There are four common types of differential reinforcement: differential reinforcement of other behavior (reinforcing the absence of the problem behavior for a specified period of time), differential reinforcement of an alternative behavior (reinforcing a specific replacement behavior while the problem behavior results in extinction), differential reinforcement of an incompatible behavior (reinforcing an alternative behavior that is physically incompatible with the target challenging behavior), and differential reinforcement of a low rate of behavior (reinforcement is provided for only engaging the problem behavior a low number of times).

A third type of consequence intervention is called punishment. Punishment is a technical term that refers to a consequence that follows a behavior and in the future the behavior decreases. Punishment, like reinforcement, can be positive (event or item added to the environment) or negative (event or item removed from the environment). Examples of positive punishment include providing things like reprimands contingent on a problem behavior. Examples of negative punishment include removing preferred things like recess, TV time, or play time contingent on a problem behavior. Punishment should only be used as a last resort intervention (after positive interventions have been exhausted, the child's behavior is a danger to self or others or significantly impacts the daily functioning of the child), and after careful consideration and appropriate regulatory approvals, as many ethical implications exist with its use.

Intervention Plan Considerations

When a plan is written to decrease a problem behavior, it may include a combination of the three types of interventions. A positive behavior support plan that uses all three strategies would comprehensively address the challenging behavior as it will decrease the likelihood that the behavior will occur, in other words, help to prevent the behavior, by using antecedent, or "A" strategies. It would also teach a functionally equivalent replacement behavior, while decreasing the future likelihood of the target behavior through "B" and "C" strategies. It is important to create a plan that is both preventative and supportive and not just reactive. If the plan only includes reactive "C" strategies, the child will not learn appropriate behavior and may find other challenging behavior to engage in for the same purposes. It should also include the name of the target behavior and its operational definition as well as the hypothesis statement from the FBA. Additionally, the plan should include the date of the development of the plan, data collection procedures for progress monitoring, safety measures, and procedures to fade the intervention as the problem behavior decreases.

Other things should be taken into consideration when an intervention plan is developed. One consideration is safety. If the problem behavior is one that poses risk of injury to the individual themselves (e.g., self-injurious behavior) or others (e.g., aggression), then safety of the individual and others should always be taken into account. Extinction may cause the behavior to increase before it decreases and if this poses risk of injury, it should be carefully considered, as should protective equipment for the individual or caregivers. In addition, ecological fit and social validity should be considered. Ecological fit involves ensuring the plan fits the environment and is able to be implemented given the training and resources of the people implementing it. Social validity refers to ensuring the intervention is acceptable to those implementing it, reasonably easy to implement, and the goals and results have value to the child's caregivers and community. Ensuring that the interventions are socially valid and fit with the environment, help to make it more likely the interventions will be implemented as written, or in other words, have a high degree of treatment integrity.

Systems and Collaboration

What Is Collaboration?

Essential to promoting the social, emotional, and behavioral needs of children with ASD is the collaboration of the individuals in their lives. This often includes teachers, parents, medical doctors, psychologists, behavior analysts, and siblings. Collaboration can have many definitions, but most definitions include key core components. The first, collaborative partners are equal; the second, collaboration is voluntary; the third, there is shared decision making between parties; and the fourth is working toward a common goal (Cook & Friend, 1991). Collaboration is not something that often occurs naturally, but rather something that requires effort and practice to put into place. A truly collaborative support system for a child with ASD is one where the individuals in the child's life are able to work together to develop appropriate skill building activities, and to promote a positive environment designed to foster growth.

Collaboration often occurs in a consultative relationship. Consultation occurs when a consultant (e.g., teacher, behavior analyst, psychologist) works with a consultee (e.g., aide, teacher, parent) toward a shared goal for the client (the child with ASD). The defining feature of consultation is that it is triadic in nature involving a consultant, consultee, and client, and that the relationship between the consultant and consultee is an equal, nonhierarchical relationship (Erchul & Sheridan, 2014). This is similar to a collaborative relationship; however, not all consultation relationships are collaborative. While more research is needed on well-defined collaboration and its impact, collaboration between home and school professionals is essential to include relevant individuals in a child's life to support the needs of the child (Cook & Friend, 2010; Miller, Colebrook, & Ellis, 2014).

Throughout this book, we have seen that the different interventions outlined have a particular focus on changing the behavior of the individuals in a child's social network in order to promote change and growth in the child. Take for example a student who was having difficulty in the playground because he was throwing the ball at the other students. Upon further analysis it might be observed that the student had difficulty initiating interaction with his peers in an effort to play the game. The best way for him to get the students attention and be invited to play the game was to throw the ball at them. After determining the function of this behavior, an intervention involved a collaborative effort with the teachers, parents, and other peers to promote appropriate initiation of play and to decrease the throwing of the ball at others. Teachers were asked to teach specific ways to initiate play, parents were asked to continue to develop this skill at home, and other peers were taught the importance of socializing with others and including them in the game.

The steps to developing a collaborative relationship occur right at the beginning of the professional relationship. Establishing a relationship with the child as well as the individuals supporting the needs of the child is the key component to successful treatment and intervention. This occurs from Day 1. The individuals responsible for developing this collaborative relationship are likely to be not only educational professionals from the home and school, but are also various clinicians and medical professionals. Adopting a CORE model of collaboration may be beneficial, one that fosters connection, optimism, respect, and empowerment (Minke, 2010).

How to Promote Relationship Development and Collaboration?

Entry Phase—Problem Identification

As the saying goes, a first impression goes a long way. The entry phase is that time during consultation and intervention development, where the clinician is getting to know the child, the parent, the teacher, the setting, and any organizational aspects of the setting that may be relevant.

This initial time during the entry phase is perhaps the most important in developing a positive relationship with all key individuals that will last throughout the process. Some activities that may help support relationship development during this time are engaging in active listening of the individuals involved; this includes paraphrasing, reflective responding, and communicating empathy. Remember this is a potentially difficult time for a parent, caregiver, or teacher who is reaching out in the best interest of the child. Listening to their concerns, fears, and past experiences is essential to moving the process forward and collaboratively identifying the problem and developing solutions in the later stages of problem analysis, intervention implementation and evaluation (Kratochwill & Bergan, 1990).

Some possible barriers that may occur during this time is a hesitancy for individuals to ask for help, a failure to see that there may be a problem, an initial hesitancy to engage in a collaborative relationship due to a past negative experience, or a possible belief that the process may reveal negative aspects about the classroom, teacher, parent, or household. To counteract some of these barriers it is important for the clinician to engage in open communication, and to outline the limits of consultation that define the specific aspects of the relationship. Be sure to not assign blame and to communicate from a place of empathy and mutual respect. Remind consultees of the shared goals between each of the parties and focus on those goals.

Problem Analysis

During the problem analysis phase of collaboration, individuals are exploring the data that are collected and determining potential hypotheses that are maintaining challenging behavior. At this time, it is important to describe the data in an objective way, but in a way that is nonaccusatory. Maintaining a collaborative relationship during this time involves coming from a place that all parties are doing the best that they can at the time. There should be a communication of positivity, specifically an optimism that when individuals involved understand how to respond a different way to the behavior that they will do so (Minke, 2010).

Remember when we are collecting data on a child's environment, we are collecting data on how the adults in the environment respond to that behavior. We may find things that could be done better or the data may reveal things that the individual was not aware they were doing. Take for example, a child with ASD who is beginning to engage in self-injury in the classroom. The data reveal that when the child is in a low attention situation and then engages in self-injury the teacher immediately comes over and talks with the student. It is important to understand that when this is communicated to the teacher that aspects of an individual's behavior may be revealed that were not realized. This should be communicated from a place of helping, empathy, and optimism.

Intervention Development and Implementation

Collaborative intervention development is key. Anyone involved in implementing an intervention should have a voice in its development. Individuals are much more likely to implement an intervention in which they have ownership and a hand in developing. Additionally, it is very important that there is accountability in the intervention implementation. Since a teacher or parent is accountable for the implementation of an intervention, they should be involved in the development. This is achieved by soliciting input from stakeholders, reflective listening of opinions, identifying barriers in the environment that may make implementation difficult, and coming to consensus on aspects of the intervention. This effective collaboration between the home and school environment has been shown to increase the effectiveness of interventions (NRC, 2001; Cho Blair et al., 2011).

Intervention Evaluation

Evaluation of intervention is crucial in determining if the child is reaching the goals collaboratively identified in the entry and analysis stages of consultation. During this time, treatment will be evaluated through the data collected by the clinician or the individual implementing the intervention. It is important to keep in mind that while this stage is evaluative, it should be treated as informative and skill developing. A consultant may find that the parent or teacher may not have been implementing the intervention as planned. This can be an uncomfortable situation to address. The conversation should come from a place of belief that the individual is doing the best that they can and feedback will likely result in improved performance. Additionally, a problem-solving approach should be adopted. There are likely a multitude of reasons an intervention is not being implemented as planned that have little to do with the individual implementing the intervention, such as the match between the intervention and the system or environment. If it is found that the reason for the lack of correct implementation are primarily due to the person implementing the intervention, then a problem-solving approach focusing on why the intervention is not being implemented as planned should be the focus. This will involve directly including all individuals responsible for the development and implementation of the intervention. The table below summarizes the collaborative steps and barriers.

	Collaborative steps	Barriers
Entry-problem identification	Relationship building Identifying mutual goals Empathy Nonhierarchical	Difficult to admit there is a problem. Time constraints Fear of change
Problem analysis	Mutual problem solving Accountability Open communication	Hesitancy to analyze own behavior System constraints
Intervention development	Skill building Training and support	Differing opinions and achieving consensus Possibly more work initially
Intervention evaluation	Supportive data collection Problem-solving approach	Evaluative Possible defensiveness

Interprofessional Collaboration

Throughout the book, we have seen the complex nature of ASD in relation to medical, behavioral, psychological, and social or emotional concerns. For this reason, interprofessional collaboration between the professionals responsible for providing care and intervention is of utmost importance. The majority of the time, a child with ASD will be provided with care from multiple professionals in a variety of different settings. Some of the clinicians involved may be responsible for the implementation and follow up of suggested interventions and treatment; however, intervention and treatment are often provided in the home and school environments with oversight by parents, teachers, school psychologists, and other caregivers.

Medical Care

Children with ASD have specific needs that will likely be addressed by medical professionals and specialists. In addition to overall care provided by a pediatrician, specific needs that could be addressed by a medical professional could include psychopharmacological medications for needs such as attention or hyperactivity. Gastrointestinal concerns that may be related to food selectivity, allergies, or lactose intolerance may be addressed by medical professionals. Additionally, if a child with ASD has seizures, then he or she may be followed by a neurologist. Any intervention should be in collaboration with medical professionals to ensure that the medical needs are addressed.

Ancillary Therapies

Specialized therapies can include speech therapy, occupational therapy, and physical therapy. Speech therapists will likely address issues related to speech productivity, articulation, expressive, and receptive language skills. Additionally, a speech therapist may work with the child on potential feeding issues related to oral motor skills. Occupational therapists address fine and gross motor skills related to academic, vocational, and life skills. Similarly, occupational therapists may provide oversight of sensory concerns by helping to support exposure and tolerance of sensory stimuli that may be avoided by the child. Physical therapists may work on problems related to physical movement such as muscle tone, balance, and coordination.

Interprofessional collaboration is defined by the World Health Organization (Gilbert, Yan, & Hoffman, 2010) as "multiple health workers from different professional backgrounds provide comprehensive services by working with patients, their families, caregivers, and communities, to deliver the highest quality of care across settings" (p. 13). As with the multiple aspect of collaboration discussed throughout this chapter, this often does not occur naturally and must be something that is worked toward. The steps involved in creating a strong interprofessional collaboration involve forming a committed team, identifying and working on a joint problem, and a clinician communicating their role effectively (Boshoff & Stewart, 2013; Peabody & Demanchich, 2016; Stein, Strohmeier, & Barthold, 2016). As this relates to a child with ASD, it is very similar to the steps of collaboration discussed earlier. It is essential that all clinician, caregivers, and stakeholders are part of a committed team, with agreed upon goals, who communicate their roles and take responsibility and accountability for their part in the treatment and intervention.

Where Do We Foster Collaboration?

A basic understanding of the systems with which an intervention will be implemented is hallmark to initiating and sustaining change. The specifics and culture of different environments need to be assessed and any specific barriers to the system should be addressed, before, during, and after intervention and treatment. These environments include the culture of the home, school, and community. Effective interventions are ones that can be generalized to the multiple environments that a child inhabits, with tweaking based on the specifics of that environment. Special attention should be paid to whether an intervention can be introduced at the universal, targeted, or individual level.

Culture of Environments

The culture of the home and school should not only be considered while developing an intervention, but steps should also be taken to improve the culture if necessary to support the intervention. Culture and climate in the home and school environments includes essential components such as safety, relationships, teaching and learning, and physical environment (Thapa et al., 2013).

Safety and physical environment should be assessed as part of intervention development and implementation. This includes the rules and norms of each environment, the physical and the emotional safety in the environment, as well as approaches to discipline. Take for example, a home environment where the rules and approaches to discipline are harsh and punitive. Steps toward educating a parent on the importance and effectiveness of positive approaches and the dangers of harsh discipline procedures should be reviewed (Gershoff, 2008). Additionally, in a classroom environment, these approaches to discipline should also be addressed as well as the aspects of physical and emotional safety. Before individualized interventions are implemented, physical and emotional safety should be ensured. If the rules and norms of the home environment are reasonable and effective, then steps should be made to implement interventions that fit within those rules and norms. Relationships between individuals in the school and home environment and respect of diversity are other essential aspects of climate to be addressed. Any treatment or intervention should be developed with respect for all of the individuals in the environment as well as the culture and norms of the family members.

Multitiered Systems of Support

When implementing an intervention in the school environment, it is important to consider the multitiered system of support (MTSS). This systems level approach to intervention separates a system out into three tiers defined as follows: Tier 1 or Universal Support, Tier 2 or Targeted Group Support, Tier 3 or Individualized Support (Sayeski & Brown, 2014). An MTSS is a prevention-oriented approach with the goal of providing the most comprehensive behavioral and instructional support at the universal levels and then providing additional supports as needed. Ideally, in a school or classroom, 80 percent of students should be responding to Universal Supports (core academic and behavioral curriculum). About 15 percent of students may need some additional supports in the form of small group instruction or increased practice, and maybe 3 to 5 percent of students may require more individualized or special education.

So how does this relate to a child with ASD? Typically, if a child with ASD is having academic, social, or behavioral difficulty that is impeding performance in school then the student will likely be classified under IDEA and have an IEP. However, just because a child is classified does not mean that an individualized plan for all skills is always necessary. Attempts should be made to develop interventions that work within the tiered systems of support. Say for example, that a teacher has a class-wide positive behavior support plan that involves specific reinforcement for respectful behavior. Within her class she has a child with ASD that is having difficulty with disruptive behavior in the classroom. If possible, and if it makes functional sense, it may be helpful to have any plan that is put in place for the child "fit" within the universal plan of the classroom.

CHAPTER 5

Case Studies

Case Study: Willie

Willie is a 4-year-old boy who lives at home with his mother, father, and 5-year-old sister. He was born at 34 weeks gestation due to maternal pre-eclampsia. He was provided care in the neonatal intensive care unit for 4 weeks following delivery. Developmental milestones were reported by his mother to be achieved within normal limits, with the exception of language development. Currently, Willie is reported to repeat words and phrases but rarely initiates communication or uses these words appropriately. With respect to receptive language, Willie appears to understand, but at times will "drift into his own world." Reports indicate that he demonstrates hypersensitivity to sounds and certain textures and may become very upset at certain noises (sirens) or textures (tags on his shirt or if his clothes unexpectedly get wet). Of concern to the parents, is that he does not appear to recognize family members such as grandparents, and barely attends to the social world around him.

Willie enjoys playing with his toys, particularly cars and action figures. His mother indicated that when he is around children of his age, he does not initiate play and does not reciprocate if other peers initiate play, he does not reciprocate. If permitted, he would spend hours in front of the television watching his favorite shows. During this time, he will engage in persistent rocking back and forth. At times, if he is denied access to something that he wants he will scream, cry, and will hit a family member (father, mother, sister) if they come into his space during the tantrum.

Willie attends a preschool for 3 days a week for 3 hours a day. His teachers notice difficulty with attention during academics, particularly, during circle time he will wander around the room, and when asked to practice coloring he will attempt to get up and play with other objects in the room. He will repeat his colors and the alphabet when asked. Willie is reported to have strengths in the area of memory and will remember where everything in a room is located. However, this can sometimes pose a problem if an object is moved from the place where he remembered it. He is very good at following his schedule, but will become upset if the schedule is changed. He is reported to have an odd prosody to his speech. Willie enjoys eating chicken nuggets, pizza, and apple juice. He will often refuse vegetables and a large variety of fruits. Parents are concerned with his nutritional needs have been attempting to supplement with vitamins.

Willie's pediatrician reports that he received an "at risk" score on the M-CHAT (Modified Checklist for Autism in Toddlers; Robins et al., 2014) and has recommended additional diagnostic testing. Additionally, she is concerned with his diet and his frequent bouts of diarrhea. During an audiology visit, Willie's hearing was reported to be within normal limits. There are no other medical concerns of note.

Case Study: Mika

Mika is a 3rd grade girl recently diagnosed with Autism Spectrum Disorder. Mika was born via vaginal delivery with no reports of complications. Developmental milestones were reported to be achieved within normal limits. Mika's mother indicated that she spoke very early and family members were often would be "shocked" by the level of her vocabulary. While gross motor skills were achieved within normal limits, reports indicated that there was a bit of a delay in displaying fine motor skills. Particularly, Mika had problems with pencil grip, graphomotor skills, and tying her shoes. As a result, she was resistant to engage in tasks that required her to use her fine motor skills. Early intervention services were provided by an occupational therapist, and there was some improvement.

Mika is in a regular education 3rd grade class at her local elementary school. She was not classified in 1st and 2nd grade and was reported to perform well academically. However, she had some behavioral difficulty during unstructured activities (lunch and recess) and specials (physical education). During these times, Mika would not engage with her peers and would sit and read a book to herself during lunch and recess. When she was prompted to engage or sit with others, she would become increasingly upset and would scream that she "just wanted to read her book!" When Mika was asked if she had any friends, she indicated that she had two friends, which were students in her class; however, she was not observed to interact with these students.

While Mika's teachers report that she performs well academically, if she does not want to engage in an activity, it is very difficult to get her to do it. She particularly does not like writing tasks and physical education class. She is often easily distracted, and during transitions from tasks she will take out her book and read. At times it is easy to get her to put her book away, but often she will refuse. She responds well to schedules, but will become very upset if there is a change in schedule, such as a school assembly. If a student unexpectedly laughs or says something in class, she may scream, "shut up," or, "stop laughing." When she does not want to complete an academic task, she will put her head down and refuse.

Mika is reported to have average intelligence, with an extremely high vocabulary. She reads at a high level, but sometimes struggles with comprehension. She does not like to engage in tasks that are challenging, but loves to engage in tasks where she excels. When Mika is discussing a topic of interest (e.g., Minecraft), she will become animated and happy during the social interaction.

Case Study: Donnie

Donnie is a 15-year-old, 9th grade student with a diagnosis of ASD and Intellectual Disability. He was born at 35 weeks gestation with birth complications that included meconium aspiration. Developmental milestones were reported to be delayed in most areas of functioning, with significant delays in speech. Donnie is nonverbal and communicates with PECS. He is able to respond to many questions and has strong receptive language skills; however, he has difficulty initiating communication with others. He engages in self-stimulatory behavior of hand flapping and loud vocalizations. He likes to be around other people and enjoys hugs and smiles from others.

Donnie's current placement is in an Autism Support/Life Skills special education classroom. He receives ancillary therapies such as Speech Therapy, Occupational Therapy, and Physical Therapy. He is described as compliant with directives and rarely engages in challenging behavior of aggression or tantrums. At times, when he is denied access to something that he wants he will scream and enter the personal space of another and attempt to push that individual out of the way. He enjoys watching cartoons and playing on his iPad.

Donnie requires some assistance and prompting with some activities of daily living, but he is able to brush his teeth, go to the bathroom, and wash his hands independently. He requires some prompting with showering, specifically washing his hair. He responds well to task analyses and lists of items (with pictures) that he should complete during these activities and others. Donnie loves to cook and be in the kitchen. He is able to identify many objects in the kitchen as well as sort those objects. He understands quantity to a certain degree, but has some difficulty if the objects are not in front of him. Socially, he enjoys being around others and others enjoy being around him.

ASD Behavior Support Plan Checklist and Planning

	Functional Behavioral Assessment (FBA)
	An FBA is conducted and includes indirect and direct assessments
	A record review is conducted including review of any previous incident reports and levels of functioning, including communication
	FBA is conducted in the natural environment or in a comparable contrived environment
	Behavior is observed in the natural setting
	Data are collected on the antecedents and consequences preceding and following the target behavior in the natural environment
	Baseline data are collected to determine problem level
	Target behaviors are prioritized and operationally defined
	Medical conditions are ruled out
	A functional analysis is conducted if needed
	Data are summarized and written in a report
	A hypothesis statement is developed
	Hypothesis is confirmed in some way

	Behavior Support Plan
	Function-based interventions are developed based on the FBA results
	Intervention plan includes operational definition of target behaviors
	Intervention plan is ecologically sound
	Safety plans are put into place
	Intervention plan includes "A" antecedent strategies
	Intervention plan includes "B" functionally equivalent replacement strategies
	Intervention plan includes "C" consequence strategies, including reinforcement for appropriate behavior and extinction for inappropriate behavior
	Intervention plan includes data collection methods for progress monitoring
	Intervention plan includes training procedures for caregivers
	Criteria for fading out or modifying interventions are developed
	Intervention plan includes strategies to promote generalization and maintenance
	Intervention plan includes a safety plan as needed

ASD Programming Checklist and Planning

	Social Skills Programming
	Assessment is conducted to determine social competency deficit areas
	Assessment is conducted to determine if deficits are due to skill deficit, performance deficit, interfering behavior, or generalization difficulties
	Goals are identified and written in observable and measurable terms
	Plan for intervention is developed, written, and trained
	Intervention includes prompting hierarchies appropriate to the student
	Intervention includes modeling (video or live)
	Intervention includes a system for reinforcement of appropriate skills
	If appropriate, peers are trained to prompt and reinforce appropriate social behavior
	Intervention plan includes teaching and practicing in the natural environment
	Intervention plan addresses any interfering behaviors
	Intervention plan includes targeting any communication difficulties
	A plan is developed to program for generalization and maintenance

	Functional Daily Living Skills
	Assessments are conducted to determine deficit areas
	Goals are identified and written in observable and measurable terms
	Task analyses are written for skills targeted
	Baseline data are collected on areas of the task analyses that are inadequate
	Forward chaining, backward chaining, or total task instructional plans are developed
	Teaching includes programming for generalization and maintenance
	Skills are taught in the natural environment
	Data are collected and analyzed regularly for progress monitoring

	Communication
	An appropriate communication modality (i.e., selection-based or topography-based) is selected for the child based on skills and preferences
	An assessment of the verbal operants is conducted to determine specific communication deficits
	Goals are identified and written in observable and measurable terms

	An instructional program is developed to target all deficit areas, starting with mands
	Instructional program is based on Skinner's analysis of verbal behavior
	All potential communicative partners are informed of the preferred communication modality and trained to model, prompt, and reinforce appropriate communication
	Communication instruction takes place in the natural environment and opportunities are both captured and contrived
	Errorless teaching is used with modeling and prompting

	Vocational
	Programming begins no later than age 16
	Assessments are conducted to determine deficit areas
	Goals are identified and written in observable and measurable terms
	Goals are based on anticipated post-21 placements
	Programming includes prompting hierarchies and modeling appropriate to the student
	Behavioral skills training is used as appropriate
	Programming occurs in the natural environment and community-based instruction is used often
	Programming includes preference-based teaching and goal selection
	Intervention plan addresses any interfering behaviors
	Intervention plan includes targeting any communication difficulties
	A plan is developed to program for generalization and maintenance
	Data are collected and analyzed regularly for progress monitoring

	Academic
	Assessments are conducted to determine deficit areas
	Assessment is conducted to determine if deficits are due to skill deficit, performance deficit, interfering behavior, or generalization difficulties
	Goals are identified and written in observable and measurable terms
	Instructional programs are developed that include prompt hierarchies, criteria for mastery or change, and so on
	Programs are written at the child's instructional level
	Errorless teaching is used
	Teaching includes programming for generalization and maintenance
	Data are collected and analyzed regularly for progress monitoring
	Discrete trial teaching and/or natural environment teaching is used as appropriate
	Instruction occurs in the least restrictive setting

References

Allen, K. D., Wallace, D. P., Greene, D. J., Bowen, S. L., & Burke, R. V. (2010). Community-based vocational instruction using videotaped modeling for young adults with autism spectrum disorders performing in air-inflated mascots. *Focus on Autism and Other Developmental Disabilities, 25,* 186–192.

American Academy of Pediatrics, Committee on Children With Disabilities. (2006). Identifying Infants and Young Children with Developmental Disorders in the Medical Home. *Pediatrics, 118*(1).

American Academy of Pediatrics. (2016). 2016 Recommendations for preventive pediatric health care. *Pediatrics, 137*(1), 1–3. doi:10.1542/peds.2015-3908

American Psychiatric Association. (1952). *Diagnostic and Statistical Manual of Mental Disorders* (1st ed.). Washington, DC: American Psychiatric Publishing.

American Psychiatric Association. (1968). *Diagnostic and Statistical Manual of Mental Disorders* (2nd ed.). Washington, DC: American Psychiatric Publishing.

American Psychiatric Association. (1980). *Diagnostic and Statistical Manual of Mental Disorders* (3rd ed.). Washington, DC: American Psychiatric Publishing.

American Psychiatric Association. (1994). *Diagnostic and Statistical Manual of Mental Disorders* (4th ed.). Washington, DC: American Psychiatric Publishing.

American Psychiatric Association. (2013). *Diagnostic and Statistical Manual of Mental Disorders* (5th ed.). Washington, DC: American Psychiatric Publishing.

APA Presidential Task Force on Evidence-Based Practice. (2006). Evidence-based practice in psychology. *American Psychologist, 61,* 271–285.

Ayres, K. M., & Langone, J. (2005). Intervention and instruction with video for students with autism: A review of the literature. *Education and Training in Developmental Disabilities, 40*(2), 183–196.

Baer, D. M., Wolf, M. M., & Risley, T. R. (1968). Some current dimensions of applied behavior analysis. *Journal of Applied Behavior Analysis, 1*(1), 91. Retrieved from www.ncbi.nlm.nih.gov/pubmed/16795165

Bailey, A., Phillips, W., & Rutter, M. (1996). Autism: Towards an integration of clinical, genetic, neuropsychological, and neurobiological perspectives. *Journal of Child Psychology and Psychiatry, and Allied Disciplines, 37*(1), 89–126. doi:10.1111/j.1469-7610.1996.tb01381.x

Bambara, L. M., Cole, C. L., Kunsch, C., Tsai, S., & Ayad, E. (2016). A peer-mediated intervention to improve the conversational skills of high school students with autism spectrum disorder. *Research in Autism Spectrum Disorders, 27*, 29–43. doi:10.1016/j.rasd.2016.03.003

Banda, D. R., Dogoe, M. S., & Matuszny, R. M. (2011). Review of video prompting studies with persons with developmental disabilities. *Education and Training in Autism and Developmental Disabilities, 46*(4), 514–527.

Beauchaine, T. P., Hinshaw, S. P. (2013). *Child and adolescent psychopathology* (2nd ed.). Hoboken, NJ: John Wiley & Sons.

Becker, R. L. (2001). *Reading-Free Vocational Interest Inventory-Second Edition* (R-FVII:2). Austin, TX: Pro-Ed.

Bellini, S. (2006). *Building Social Relationships: A Systematic Approach to Teaching Social Interaction Skills to Children and Adolescents with Autism Spectrum Disorders and Other Social Difficulties.* AAPC Publishing.

Blair, K. S. C., Lee, I., Cho, S., & Dunlap, G. (2011). Positive behavior support through Family School collaboration for young children with autism. *Topics in Early Childhood Special Education, 31*(1), 22–36. doi:10.1177/0271121410377510

Bondy, A., & Frost, L. (2001). The picture exchange communication system. *Behavior Modification, 25*, 725–744.

Bondy, A., Tincani, M., & Frost, L. (2004). Multiply controlled verbal operants: An analysis and extension to the picture exchange communication system. *The Behavior Analyst/MABA, 27*(2), 247–261. Retrieved from www.ncbi.nlm.nih.gov/pubmed/22478433

Boshoff, K., & Stewart, H. (2013). Key principles for confronting the challenges of collaboration in educational settings. *Australian Occupational Therapy Journal, 60*(2), 144–147. doi:10.1111/1440-1630.12003

Browder, D. M., Snell, M. E., & Wildonger, B. A. (1988). Simulation and community-based instruction of vending machines with time delay. *Education and Training in Mental Retardation, 23*(3), 175–185.

Chang, Y., & Locke, J. (2016). A systematic review of peer-mediated interventions for children with autism spectrum disorder. *Research in Autism Spectrum Disorders, 27*, 1–10. doi:10.1016/j.rasd.2016.03.010

Chess, S., Fernandez, P. B., & Korn, S. J. (1971). *Psychiatric Disorders of Children with Congenital Rubella.* New York, NY: Brunner/Mazel.

Christensen, D. L., Baio, J., Braun, K. V. N., Bilder, D., Charles, J., Constantino, J. N., Daniels, J., Durkin, M. S., Fitzgerald, R. T., Kurzius-Spencer, M., Lee, L. -C., Pettygrove, S., Robinson, C., Schulz, E., Wells, C., Wingate, M.S., Zahorodny, W., Yeargin-Allsopp, M. (2016). Prevalence and characteristics of autism spectrum disorder among children aged 8 years—Autism and developmental disabilities monitoring network, 11 sites, United States, 2012. *Surveillance Summaries, 65*(3), 1–23. doi:www.cdc.gov/mmwr/volumes/65/ss/ss6503a1.htm

Cipani, E., & Schock, K. M. (2011). *Functional behavioral assessment, diagnosis, and treatment* (2nd ed.). New York, NY: Springer.

Committee for Children. 2017. *Second Step SEL Program.* Seattle, WA; Committee for Children.

Constantino, J. N. (2005). *Social Responsiveness Scale.* Torrence, CA: WPS.

Cook, L., & Friend, M. (1991). Principles for the practice of collaboration in schools. *Preventing School Failure: Alternative Education for Children and Youth, 35*(4), 6–9. doi:10.1080/1045988X.1991.9944251

Cook, L., & Friend, M. (2010). The state of the art of collaboration on behalf of students with disabilities. *Journal of Educational and Psychological Consultation, 20*(1), 1–8. doi:10.1080/10474410903535398

Cooper, J.O., Heron, T.E., & Heward, W.L. (2007). *Applied Behavior Analysis* (2nd ed.). Harlow, United Kingdom: Pearson/Merrill-Prentice Hall.

Daly, E. J., Witt, J. C., Martens, B. K., & Dool, E. J. (1997). A model for conducting a functional analysis of academic performance problems. *School Psychology Review, 26*(4), 554–574.

Delano, M. E. (2007). Video modeling interventions for individuals with autism. *Remedial and Special Education, 28*(1), 33–42.

DeLeon, I. G., & Iwata, B. A. (1996). Evaluation of a multiple-stimulus presentation format for assessing reinforcer preferences. *Journal of Applied Behavior Analysis, 29*(4), 519–533. doi:10.1901/jaba.1996.29-519

DeStefano, F., Price, C. S., & Weintraub, E. S. (2013). Increasing exposure to antibody-stimulating proteins and polysaccharides in vaccines is not associated with risk of autism. *The Journal of Pediatrics, 163*(2), 561–567. doi:10.1016/j.jpeds.2013.02.001

Durand, V. M. (1999). Functional communication training using assistive devices: Recruiting natural communities of reinforcement. *Journal of Applied Behavior Analysis, 32*(3), 247–267.

Durand, V. M., & Crimmins, D. B. (1988). Identifying the variables maintaining self-injurious behavior. *Journal of Autism and Developmental Disorders, 18*(1), 99–117. doi:10.1007/BF02211821

Dynamic Measurement Group. (2008). *DIBELS 6th Edition Technical Adequacy Information (Tech. Rep. No. 6).* Eugene, OR: http://dibels.org/pubs.html

Engelmann, S., & Carnine, D. W. (1982). *Theory of instruction.* New York, NY: Irvington.

Erchul, W. P., & Sheridan, S. M. (2014). *Handbook of research in school consultation.* Hoboken, NJ: Routledge Ltd—M.U.A. doi:10.4324/9781315759623

Fernell, E., Eriksson, M. A., & Gillberg, C. (2013). Early diagnosis of autism and impact on prognosis: A narrative review. *Clinical Epidemiology, 5*(1), 33–43. doi:10.2147/CLEP.S41714

Fisher, W. W., Piazza, C. C., Bowman, L. G., & Amari, A. (1996). Integrating caregiver report with systematic choice assessment to enhance reinforcer identification. *American Journal of Mental Retardation: AJMR, 101*(1), 15. Retrieved from www.ncbi.nlm.nih.gov/pubmed/8827248

Fisher, W. W., Piazza, C. C., Cataldo, M. F., Harrell, R., Jefferson, G., & Conner, R. (1993). Functional communication training with and without extinction and punishment. *Journal of Applied Behavior Analysis, 26*(1), 23–36.

Friend, M. P. (1992). *Interactions: Collaboration skills for school professionals.* United States: Retrieved from http://catalog.hathitrust.org/Record/00280 9700

Frost, L., & Bondy, A. (2002). *The Picture Exchange Communication System Training Manual* (2nd ed.). Newark, DE: Pyramid Educational Products.

Ganz, J. B., Davis, J. L., Lund, E. M., Goodwyn, F. D., & Simpson, R. L. (2012). Meta-analysis of PECS with individuals with ASD: Investigation of targeted versus non-targeted outcomes, participant characteristics, and implementation phase. *Research in Developmental Disabilities, 33*(2), 406–418. doi:10.1016/j.ridd.2011.09.023

Gardener, H., Spiegelman, D., & Buka, S. L. (2009). Prenatal risk factors for autism: Comprehensive meta-analysis. *The British Journal of Psychiatry, 195*(1), 7–14. doi:10.1192/bjp.bp.108.051672

Gardener, H., Spiegelman, D., & Buka, S. L. (2011). Perinatal and neonatal risk factors for autism: A comprehensive Meta-analysis. *Pediatrics, 128*(2), pp. 344–355. doi:10.1542/peds.2010-1036

Gentry, T., Wallace, J., Kvarfordt, C., & Lynch, K. B. (2010). Personal digital assistants as cognitive aids for high school students with autism: Results of a community-based trial. *Journal of Vocational Rehabilitation, 32*(2), 101–107.

Gershoff, E. T. (2008). *Report on Physical Punishment in the United States: What Research Tells Us About Its Effects on Children.* Columbus, OH: Center for Effective Discipline.

Gilbert, J. H. V., Yan, J., & Hoffman, S. J. (2010). A WHO report: Framework for action on interprofessional education and collaborative practice. *Journal of Allied Health, 39*(3), 196. Retrieved from http://search.proquest.com/docview/874211186

Gilliam, J. E. (2014). Gilliam Autism Rating Scale, Third Edition. Austin, TX: Pro-Ed, Inc.

Goldsmith, T. R., & LeBlanc, L. A. (2004). Use of technology in interventions for children with autism. *Journal of Early and Intensive Behavior Intervention, 1*(2), 166–178.

Grafodatskaya, D., Chung, B., Szatmari, P., & Weksberg, R. (2010) Autism spectrum disorders and Epigenetics. *Journal of the American Academy of Child & Adolescent Psychiatry, 49*(8), 794–809. doi:10.1016/j.jaac.2010.05.005

Graves, T. B., Collins, B. C., Schuster, J. W., & Kleinert, H. (2005). Using video prompting to teach cooking skills to secondary students with moderate disabilities. *Education and Training in Developmental Disabilities, 40*(1), 34–46.

Gresham, F. M., & Elliot, S. N. (1990). *Social Skills Rating System (SSRS).* Circle Pines, MN: American Guidance Service.

Gresham, F. M., & Elliot, S. N. (2008). *Social Skills Improvement System Rating Scales (SSIS).* San Antonio, TX; Pearson.

Hagopian, L. P., Fisher, W. W., Sullian, M., Thibault, A, J., & LeBlanc, L. A. (1998). Effectiveness of functional communication training with and without extinction and punishment: A summary of 21 inpatient cases. *Journal of Applied Behavior Analysis, 31*(2), 211–235.

Halfon, N., & Kuo, A. A. (2013). What DSM-5 could mean to children with autism and their families. *JAMA Pediatrics, 167*(7), 608. Retrieved from www.ncbi.nlm.nih.gov/pubmed/23645093

Harms, M., Martin, A., & Wallace, G. (2010). Facial emotion recognition in autism spectrum disorders: A review of behavioral and neuroimaging studies. *Neuropsychology Review, 20(3),* 290–322.

Hendricks, D., & Wehman, P. (2009). Transition from school to adulthood for youth with autism spectrum disorders. *Focus on Autism and Other Developmental Disabilities, 24*(2), 77–88. doi:10.1177/1088357608329827

Hops, J. (2008). Best practices in aligning academic assessment with instruction. In A. Thomas & J. Grimes (Eds.), *Best Practices in School Psychology V.* Bethesda, MD: National Association of School Psychologists.

Ingram, K., Lewis-Palmer, T., & Sugai, G. (2005). Function-based intervention planning. *Journal of Positive Behavior Interventions, 7*(4), 224–236. doi:10.11 77/10983007050070040401

Iwata, B. A., Deleon, I. G., & Roscoe, E. M. (2013). Reliability and validity of the functional analysis screening tool. *Journal of Applied Behavior Analysis, 46*(1), 271. doi:10.1002/jaba.31

Iwata, B. A., Dorsey, M. F., Slifer, K. J., Bauman, K. E., & Richman, G. S. (1982/1994). Toward a functional analysis of self-injury. *Journal of Applied Behavior Analysis, 27*(2), 197–209. doi:10.1901/jaba.1994.27-197

Jacobson, J. W., Mulick, J. A., & Green, G. (1998). Cost–benefit estimates for early intensive behavioral intervention for young children with autism— General model and single state case. *Behavioral Interventions, 13*(4), 201–226. doi:AID-BIN17>3.3.CO;2-I

Johnson, C. P., and Myers, S. M. (2007). Identification and evaluation of children with Autism Spectrum Disorders. *Pediatrics, 120*(5), 1183–1215. doi: 10.1542/peds.2007-2361

Klose, L., Plotts, C., Kozeneski, N., & Skinner-Foster, J. (2012). A review of assessment tools for diagnosis of autism spectrum disorders: Implications for school practice. *Assessment for Effective Intervention, 37*(4), 236–242. doi:10.1177/1534508411415090

Kluth, P. (2000). Community-referenced learning and the inclusive classroom. *Remedial and Special Education, 21*(1), 19–26.

Koegel, R. I., & Frea, W. D. (1993). Treatment of social behavior in autism through the modification of pivotal social skills. *Journal of Applied Behavior Analysis, 26*(3), 369–377.

Krakowiak, P., Walker, C. K., Bremer, A. A., Baker, A. S., Ozonoff, S., Hansen, R. L., & Hertz-Picciotto, I. (2012). Maternal metabolic conditions and risk for autism and other neurodevelopmental disorders. *Pediatrics, 129*(5), e1128. doi:10.1542/peds.2011-2583

Kratochwill, T. R., & Bergan, J. R. (1990). Behavioral consultation in applied settings: An individual guide. New York: Plenum Press.

Lamarre, J., & Holland, J. G. (1985). The functional independence of mands and tacts. *Journal of the Experimental Analysis of Behavior, 43*(1), 5–19. doi:10.1901/jeab.1985.43-5

Lovaas, O. I. (1987). Behavioral treatment and normal educational and intellectual functioning in young autistic children. *Journal of Consulting and Clinical Psychology, 55*(1), 3–9. doi:10.1037/0022-006X.55.1.3

Martens, B.K., DiGennaro, F.D., Reed, D.D., Szczech, F.M., & Rosenthal, B.D. (2008). Contingency space analysis: An alternative method for identifying contingent relations from observational data. *Journal of Applied Behavior Analysis, 41*, 69–81.

Maurice, C., Green, G., & Luce, S. (Eds.). (1996). *Behavioral Interventions for Young Children with Autism: A Manual for Parents and Professionals.* Austin, TX: Pro-Ed.

McCoy, K., & Hermansen, E. (2007). Video modeling for individuals with autism: A review of model types and effects. *Education and Treatment of Children, 30*, 183–213.

McEachin, J. J., Smith, T., & Lovaas, O. I. (1993). Long-term outcome for children with autism who received early intensive behavioral treatment. *American Journal of Mental Retardation: AJMR, 97*(4), 359. Retrieved from www.ncbi.nlm.nih.gov/pubmed/8427693

McGinnis, E., Simpson, R. L. (2016). *Skillstreaming Children and Youth with High Functioning Autism: A Guide for Teaching Prosocial Skills.* Champaign, IL; Research Press, Co.

Miller, G. E., Colebrook, J., & Ellis, B. R. (2014). Advocating for the rights of the child through family–school collaboration. *Journal of Educational and Psychological Consultation, 24*(1), 10–27. doi:10.1080/10474412.2014.870 483

Minke, K. M. (2010). Helping teachers develop productive working relationships with families: The CORE model of family-school collaboration. *International Journal for School-Based Family Counseling, 2*(1), 1–13. Retrieved: www.schoolbasedfamilycounseling.com/journal.html)

National Academies of Sciences, Engineering, and Medicine. (2015). *Mental Disorders and Disabilities Among Low-Income Children.* Washington, DC: The National Academies Press.

National Autism Center. (2015). *National Standards Report.* Randolph: National Autism Center.

National Research Council. (2001). *Educating Children with Autism.* Committee on Educational Interventions for Children with Autism. Catherine Lord and James P. McGee, eds. Division of Behavioral and Social Sciences and Education. Washington, DC: National Academy Press.

Newcomer, L., & Lewis, T. (2004). Functional behavioral assessment. *Journal of Emotional and Behavioral Disorders, 12*(3), 168–181. doi:10.1177/10634266040120030401

Newell, A. R. (2006). Controversial Therapies for Developmental Disabilities: Fad, Fashion, and Science in Professional Practice. Edited by John W. Jacobson, Richard M. Foxx, and James A. Mulick; Mahwah, New Jersey, Lawrence Erlbaum Associates.

Nuernberger, J. E., Ringdahl, J. E., Vargo, K. K., Crumpecker, A. C., & Gunnarsson, K. F. (2013). Using a behavioral skills training package to teach conversation skills to young adults with autism spectrum disorders. *Research in Autism Spectrum Disorders, 7*(2), 411–417.

O'Neill, R. E., Albin, R. W., Horner, R. H., Storey, K., & Sprague, J. R. (2015). *Functional Assessment and Program Development for Problem Behavior* (2nd ed.). Pacific Grove, CA: Brooks/Cole.

Otero, T. L., Schatz, R. B., Merrill, A. C., & Bellini, S. (2015). Social skills training for youth with autism spectrum disorders: A follow-up. *Child and Adolescent Psychiatric Clinics of North America, 24*(1), 99. Retrieved from www.ncbi.nlm.nih.gov/pubmed/25455578

Ozonoff, S. (2010). A prospective study of the emergence of early behavioral signs of autism. *Journal of the American Academy of Child Adolescent Psychiatry, 49*(3), 266.e2. doi:10.1016/j.jaac.2009.11.009

Palmen, A., & Didden, R. (2012). Task engagement in young adults with high-functioning autism spectrum disorders: Generalization effects of behavioral skills training. *Research in Autism Spectrum Disorders, 6*(4), 1377–1388.

Palmen, A., Didden, R., & Korzilius, H. (2010). Effectiveness of behavioral skills training on staff performance in a job training setting for high-functioning adolescents with autism spectrum disorders. *Research in Autism Spectrum Disorders, 4*(4), 731–740.

Paone, J. A., & Meyer, L. S. (2009). *Connecting with Autism: A Blueprint for Lifetime Support.* Robbinsville, NJ: Autism New Jersey. Retrieved: www.autismnj.org/document.doc?id=25

Partington, J. W. (2006). *ABLLS-R-Assessment of Basic Language and Learning Skills* (revised ed.). Behavior Analysts, Inc.

Partington, J. W., & Mueller, M. M. (2012). *Assessment of Functional Living Skills.* Walnut Creek, CA: Behavior Analysts, Inc. & Stimulus Publications.

Peabody, M. A., & Demanchick, S. P. (2016). Interprofessional opportunities: Understanding roles in collaborative practice. *International Journal of Play Therapy, 25*(2), 102–111. doi:10.1037/pla0000013

Pierce, K., Carter, C., Weinfeld, M., Desmond, J., Hazin, R., Bjork, R., & Gallagher, N. (2011). Detecting, studying, and treating autism early: The one-year well-baby check-up approach. *The Journal of Pediatrics, 159*(3), 465. e6. doi:10.1016/j.jpeds.2011.02.036

Potter, B., & Brown, D. L. (1997). A review of studies examining the nature of selection-based and topography-based verbal behavior. *The Analysis of Verbal Behavior, 14*, 85–104. Retrieved from www.ncbi.nlm.nih.gov/pubmed/22477121

Ramdoss, S., Lang, R., Mulloy, A., Franco J., O'Reilly M., Didden R., & Lancioni G. (2011). Use of computer-based interventions to teach communication skills to children with autism spectrum disorders: a systematic review. *Journal of Behavioral Education, 20*(1), 55–76.

Robins, D. L., Casagrande, K., Barton, M., Chen, C. A., Dumont-Mathieu, T., & Fein, D. (2014). Validation of the modified checklist for autism in toddlers, revised with follow-up (M-CHAT-R/F). *Pediatrics, 133*(1), 37–45. doi:10.1542/peds.2013-1813

Rosenblatt, A. I., & Carbone, P. S. (2012). *Autism Spectrum Disorders: What Every Parent Needs to Know.* New York, NY: American Academy of Pediatrics.

Roullet, F. I., Lai, J. K. Y., & Foster, J. A. (2013). In utero exposure to valproic acid and autism—a current review of clinical and animal studies. *Neurotoxicology and Teratology, 36*, 47–56. doi:10.1016/j.ntt.2013.01.004

Roux, A. M., Shattuck, P. T., Rast, J. E., Rava, J. A., & Anderson, K. A. (2015). *National Autism Indicators Report: Transition into Young Adulthood.* Philadelphia, PA: Life Course Outcomes Research Program, A.J. Drexel Autism Institute, Drexel University.

Rutter, M., & LeCouteur, A. (2003). *Autism Diagnostic Interview-Revised.* Torrance, CA: Western Psychological Services.

Sayeski, K., & Brown, M. (2014). Developing a classroom management plan using a tiered approach. *Teaching Exceptional Children, 47*(2), 119–127. Retrieved from http://search.proquest.com/docview/1626814077

Schaaf, R., & Lane, A. (2015). Toward a best-practice protocol for assessment of sensory features in ASD. *Journal of Autism and Developmental Disorders, 45*(5), 1380–1395. doi:10.1007/s10803-014-2299-z

Shafer, E. (1995). A review of interventions to teach a mand repertoire. *Analysis of Verbal Behavior, 12*, 53–66.

Shelton, J. F., Hertz-Picciotto, I., & Pessah, I. N. (2012). Tipping the balance of autism risk: Potential mechanisms linking pesticides and autism. *Environmental Health Perspectives, 120*(7), 944–951. doi:10.1289/ehp.1104553

Shillingsburg, M. A., Bowen, C. N., & Shapiro, S. K. (2014). Increasing social approach and decreasing social avoidance in children with autism spectrum disorder during discrete trial training. *Research in Autism Spectrum Disorders, 8*(11), 1443–1453. doi:10.1016/j.rasd.2014.07.013

Simonoff, E., Pickles, A., Charman, T., Chandler, S., Loucas, T., & Baird, G. (2008). Psychiatric disorders in children with autism spectrum disorders: Prevalence, comorbidity, and associated factors in a population-derived sample. *Journal American Academy Child Adolescent Psychiatry, 47*(8), 921–929. doi:10.1097/CHI.0b013e318179964f

Skinner, B. F. (1957). *Verbal behavior.* New York, NY: Appleton-Century-Crofts.

Smith, R. G., & Churchill, R. M. (2002). Identification of environmental determinants of behavior disorders through functional analysis of precursor behaviors. *Journal of Applied Behavior Analysis, 35*(2), 125–136. doi:10.1901/jaba.2002.35-125

Smith, T. (2001). Discrete trial training in the treatment of autism. *Focus on Autism and Other Developmental Disabilities, 16*(2), 86–92. doi:10.1177/108835760101600204

Smith, T., & Lovaas, I. O. (1998). Intensive and early behavioral intervention with autism. *Infants & Young Children, 10*(3), 67–78. doi:10.1097/00001163-199801000-00010

Smith, T., Eikeseth, S., Klevstrand, M., & Lovaas, O. I. (1997). Intensive behavioral treatment for preschoolers with severe mental retardation and pervasive developmental disorder. *American Journal of Mental Retardation, 102*(3), 238. Retrieved from www.ncbi.nlm.nih.gov/pubmed/9394133

Sparrow, S. S., Cicchetti, D. V., & Balla, D. A. (2005). *Vineland Adaptive Behavior Scales* (2nd ed.). Circle Pines, MN: American Guidance Service.

Sparrow, S. S., Cicchetti, D. V., & Saulnier, C. A. (2016). *Vineland Adaptive Behavior Scales* (3rd ed.). Pearson.

Stein, S., Strohmeier, C., & Barthold, C. H. (2016). Working with children and working with schools. In I. L. Rubin, J. Merrick, D. E. Greydanus, D. R. Patel (Eds.), *Health Care for People with Intellectual and Developmental Disabilities Across the Lifespan.* Switzerland, Springer International. doi:10.1007/978-3-319-18096-0_130

Stewart, K. K., Carr, J. E., & LeBlanc, L. A. (2007). Evaluation of family-implemented behavioral skills training for teaching social skills to a child with Asperger's disorder. *Clinical Case Studies, 6*(3), 252–262.

Stokes, T. F., & Baer, D. M. (1977). An implicit technology of generalization. *Journal of Applied Behavior Analysis, 10*(2), 349. Retrieved from www.ncbi.nlm.nih.gov/pubmed/16795561

Stone, W. L., Coonrod, E. E., Turner, L. M., & Pozdol, S. L. (2004). Psychometric Properties of the Stat for Early Autism Screening. *Journal of Autism and Developmental Disorders, 34*, 691–701.

Sulzer-Azaroff, B., Hoffman, A., Horton, C., Bondy, A., & Frost, L. (2009). The picture exchange communication system (PECS). *Focus on Autism and Other Developmental Disabilities, 24*(2), 89–103. doi:10.1177/1088357609332743

Sundberg, M. L. (2008). *Verbal behavior milestones assessment and placement program: The VB-MAPP.* Concord, CA: AVB Press.

Sundberg, M. L., & Partington, J. (1998). *Teaching Language to Children with Autism or Other Developmental Disabilities.* Danville, CA: Behavior Analysts, Inc.

Sundberg, M. L., & Sundberg, C. T. (1990). Comparing topography-based verbal behavior with stimulus selection-based verbal behavior. *Analysis Verbal Behavior, 6*, 31–41.

Sundberg, M., & Michael, J. (2001). The benefits of skinner's analysis of verbal behavior for children with autism. *Behavior Modification, 25*(5), 698–724. doi:10.1177/0145445501255003

Szatmari, P., Jones, M. B., Tuff, L., Bartolucci, G., Fisman, S., & Mahoney, W. (1993). Lack of cognitive impairment in first-degree relatives of children with pervasive developmental disorders. *Journal of the American Academy of Child & Adolescent Psychiatry, 32*(6), 1264–1273. doi:10.1097/00004583-199311000-00022

Tarbox, J., Wallace, M. D., Tarbox, R. S. F., Landaburu, H. J., & Williams, W. L. (2004). Functional analysis and treatment of low rate problem behavior in individuals with developmental disabilities. *Behavioral Interventions, 19*(3), 187–204. doi:10.1002/bin.158

Tawney, J. W., & Gast, D. L. (1984). *Single Subject Research in Special Education.* Columbus, OH: Merrill.

Taylor, L. E., Swerdfeger, A. L., & Eslick, G. D. (2014). Vaccines are not associated with autism: An evidence-based meta-analysis of case-control and cohort studies. *Vaccine, 32*(29), 3623–3629. doi:10.1016/j.vaccine.2014.04.085

Thapa, A., Cohen, J., Guffey, S., & Higgins-D'Alessandro, A. (2013). A review of school climate research. *Review of Educational Research, 83*(3), 357–385. Retrieved from http://search.proquest.com/docview/1419774853

The Editors of The Lancet. (2010). Retraction—Ileal-lymphoid-nodular hyperplasia, non-specific colitis, and pervasive developmental disorder in children. *The Lancet, 375*(9713), 445. doi:10.1016/S0140-6736(10)60175-4

Thomason-Sassi, J. L., Iwata, B. A., Neidert, P. L., & Roscoe, E. M. (2011). Response latency as an index of response strength during functional analyses of problem behavior. *Journal of Applied Behavior Analysis, 44*(1), 51–67. doi:10.1901/jaba.2011.44-51

Trottier, G., Srivastava, L., & Walker, C. D. (1999). Etiology of infantile autism: A review of recent advances in genetic and neurobiological research. *Journal of Psychiatry & Neuroscience, 24*(2), 103–115. Retrieved from www.ncbi.nlm. nih.gov/pubmed/10212552

US department of Education. (2016). *National Center for Education Statistics.* Retrieved from https://nces.ed.gov/fastfacts/display.asp?id=64

Verhoeff, B. (2013). Autism in flux: A history of the concept from leo kanner to DSM-5. *History of Psychiatry, 24*(4), 442–458. doi:10.1177/0957154X 13500584

Volkmar, F. R., Rogers, J., Paul, R., Pelphrey, K. A., & Rogers, S. J. (2014). *Handbook of Autism and Pervasive Developmental Disorders, Diagnosis, Development, and Brain Mechanisms.* Edited by MD Fred R Volkmar (4th ed.). Hoboken, NJ: Wiley.

Vollmer, T. R., Borrero, J. C., Wright, C. S., Van Camp, C., & Lalli, J. S. (2001). Identifying possible contingencies during descriptive analyses of severe behavior disorders. *Journal of Applied Behavior Analysis, 34,* 269–287.

Wacker, D. P., Steege, M. W., Northup, J., Sasso, G. M., Berg, W., Reimers, T., Cooper, L., Cigrand, K., & Donn, L. (1990). A component analysis of functional communication training across three topographies of severe behavior problems. *Journal of Applied Behavior Analysis, 23*(4), 417–429.

Wang, S., Cui, Y., & Parrila, R. (2011). Examining the effectiveness of peer-mediated and video-modeling social skills interventions for children with autism spectrum disorders: A meta-analysis in single-case research using HLM. *Research in Autism Spectrum Disorders, 5*(1), 562–569. doi:10.1016/j. rasd.2010.06.023

Webster-Stratton, C. (2005). *The Incredible Years.* Seattle, WA; Incredible Years, Inc.

Wehman, P. (2012). *Life Beyond the Classroom: Transition Strategies for Young People with Disabilities* (2nd ed.). Baltimore, MD: Paul H. Brooks Publishing.

Wetherby, A. M. (2003). *Infant-Toddler Checklist and Easy-Score User's Guide.* United States: Retrieved from http://catalog.hathitrust.org/Record/009751787

Wing, L., Leekam, S. R., Libby, S. J., Gould, J., & Larcombe, M. (2002). The Diagnostic Interview for Social and Communication Disorders: Background, Inter-rater Reliability and Clinical Use. *Journal of Child Psychology and Psychiatry, 43*(3), 307–25.

World Health Organization. (1992). *The ICD-10 Classification of Mental and Behavioural Disorders: Clinical Descriptions and Diagnostic Guidelines.* Geneva: World Health Organization.

Zerbo, O., Iosif, A., Delwiche, L., Walker, C., & Hertz-Picciotto, I. (2011). Month of conception and risk of autism. *Epidemiology, 22*(4), 469–475. doi:10.1097/EDE.0b013e31821d0b53

Zerbo, O., Iosif, A., Walker, C., Ozonoff, S., Hansen, R., & Hertz-Picciotto, I. (2013). Is maternal influenza or fever during pregnancy associated with autism or developmental delays? Results from the CHARGE (childhood autism risks from genetics and environment) study. *Journal of Autism and Developmental Disorders, 43*(1), 25–33. doi:10.1007/s10803-012-1540-x

About the Authors

Dr Jessica Glass Kendorski, PhD, NCSP, BCBA-D, is an Associate Professor and Director of the MS programs in School Psychology and Applied Behavior Analysis at the Philadelphia College of Osteopathic Medicine (PCOM). She received her PhD in School Psychology from the APA-accredited program at Temple University. She is a licensed psychologist in Pennsylvania, and maintains certifications as a Board Certified Behavior Analyst (BCBA) and School Psychologist nationally (NCSP) and in New Jersey. Her primary research interest and expertise focus on supporting the social, emotional, and behavioral development of children diagnosed with neurodevelopmental disorders in the home, school, and residential settings. In addition, she actively works with school districts to improve systems for all students through the reform of school and district-wide academic and behavioral policies and practices. Dr Kendorski has led the development of the Applied Behavior Analysis programs at PCOM as well as the approval of these programs by the Behavior Analyst Certification Board (BACB). Prior to her position at PCOM, she was a Senior Educational Consultant at the May Institute, where she partnered with, and supported local school districts in the implementation of school and district-wide Positive Behavior Support Initiatives. Additionally, she worked at a Neurobehavioral Stabilization Program, a residential program specializing in treating children with autism and other developmental disabilities to overcome severe behavioral challenges. An appreciative mom of two, she is passionate about child advocacy, education, and positive parenting practices.

Amanda Guld Fisher, PhD, BCBA-D, earned her master's degree in psychology from the University of North Carolina Wilmington and her doctorate in Applied Behavior Analysis and Special Education from the Ohio State University. Amanda first received her board certification in behavior analysis (currently BCBA-D) in March of 2007. She has presented research at local and national conferences in a variety of subject areas including: response chains, stimulus equivalence, analysis of verbal behavior, college teaching strategies, feeding disorders, functional assessment methodology, reinforcer qualities and dimensions, communication modalities, staff training, and the treatment of challenging behavior. She has experience in staff and parent training, school consultation, developing and conducting community workshops in Applied Behavior Analysis and Autism Spectrum Disorders, conducting functional assessments and analyses, treating feeding disorders and developing and implementing behavior change procedures to address severe challenging behavior and academic deficits for individuals with autism and other developmental disabilities. Amanda is currently an Assistant Professor at Temple University in the College of Education where she teaches and advises students, and coordinates the master's degree and certificate program in ABA.

Amanda has also served as an adjunct faculty at Caldwell College, St. Joseph's University, University of Massachusetts, Boston, Temple University, and Rowan University. Previously, Amanda served as the Director of Professional Development, Training, and Research at Melmark where she directed the internal clinical training of staff, coordinated internships and BCBA supervision, coordinated research, served as a senior clinician for a caseload of children, and coordinated a 6-course BACB-approved certificate program taught at Melmark through Temple University.

Index

OTHER TITLES IN THIS CHILD CLINICAL PSYCHOLOGY "NUTS AND BOLTS" COLLECTION

Samuel T. Gontkovsky, *Editor*

Learning Disabilities
by Charles J. Golden, Lisa K. Lashley, Jared S. Link,
Matthew Zusman, Maya Pinjala, Christopher Tirado, and Amber Deckard

Elimination Disorders: Evidence-Based Treatment for Enuresis and Encopresis
by Thomas M. Reimers

Depression in Childhood and Adolescence: A Guide for Practitioners
by Rebecca A. Schwartz-Mette, Hannah R. Lawrence,
Douglas W. Nangle, Cynthia A. Erdley, Laura Andrews,
and Melissa Jankowski

Pediatric Bipolar Spectrum Disorders
by Elizabeth Burney Hamilton, Kristie Knows His Gun,
and Christina Tuning

Momentum Press is one of the leading book publishers in the field of engineering, mathematics, health, and applied sciences. Momentum Press offers over 30 collections, including Aerospace, Biomedical, Civil, Environmental, Nanomaterials, Geotechnical, and many others.

Momentum Press is actively seeking collection editors as well as authors. For more information about becoming an MP author or collection editor, please visit http://www.momentumpress.net/contact

---

Announcing Digital Content Crafted by Librarians

Momentum Press offers digital content as authoritative treatments of advanced engineering topics by leaders in their field. Hosted on ebrary, MP provides practitioners, researchers, faculty, and students in engineering, science, and industry with innovative electronic content in sensors and controls engineering, advanced energy engineering, manufacturing, and materials science.

Momentum Press offers library-friendly terms:

- perpetual access for a one-time fee
- no subscriptions or access fees required
- unlimited concurrent usage permitted
- downloadable PDFs provided
- free MARC records included
- free trials

The **Momentum Press** digital library is very affordable, with no obligation to buy in future years.

For more information, please visit **www.momentumpress.net/library** or to set up a trial in the US, please contact **mpsales@globalepress.com**.

www.ingramcontent.com/pod-product-compliance
Lightning Source LLC
Chambersburg PA
CBHW050531270326
41926CB00015B/3175